I taught them to cook

Jenny Ridgwell

A memoir of teaching and living in London in 1970s

First published by Ridgwell Press 2021

First Edition

Cover layout design by Simon Ridgwell ©Ridgwell Press
A catalogue record of this book is available from the British Library

Ridgwell Press Lewes BN7 1YY

ISBN: 9798749174243 (paperback)
Ebook addition ©April 2021 I

The Autumn Term 1972

Spag bog

'Class! Today we're making a new dish – spaghetti bolognese. On the TV, the cook Zena Skinner said you throw the spaghetti at the wall and if it's cooked it will stick.'

'Yuk' comes a mumble from the stools around my table. I'm their new cookery teacher and they're testing me out. They don't know yet that I've never cooked spaghetti before. Never eaten it either. There's a lot else they don't know about me but I'm not sharing secrets. Not yet and probably not ever at school.

'You can't buy spaghetti around here so I've bought some from a shop near me. You've probably eaten Heinz spaghetti in a tin, but this is different.'

Should I compare the choices in their east London shops to the plentiful offerings from Turkish and Caribbean stalls near my Hampstead flat?

I tip out the golden strands from a long cylinder of dark blue paper with an Italian label.

'Not eating that.' mutters a lumpen boy from one of the stools.

Bert is a name that I learnt in my first few days. He said he'd rather go fishing than come to school and never ever chose to be in my classes.

'Listen Bert. Watch as I make the bolognese. Just four ingredients – mince, lard, onions and tomato ketchup.'

'Me dad won't eat that. He'll give it to the dog.'

'Class. Gather round my gas cooker and watch me cook.'

I melt a lump of lard in a frying pan, brown the mince and onions, then blob in red tomato ketchup and enough water for the sauce. Lid on and simmer. Fancy ingredients like garlic, tomato purée and oregano are off the menu – I'm not risking more Yuks today.

The large saucepan of water is boiling on the gas ring.

'Stand back and I'll show you how the spaghetti cooks. Italians have been doing this for years. It's easy.'

I push long stiff strands into the steaming water. Bits snap off and it takes ages to soften. It looks so easy on TV.

'Class – get ready and I'll call you when my spaghetti is done.'

They clatter out equipment and measure ingredients.

'Come and watch.'

Just like the TV cook, I fork out a long pasta strand and fling it at the wall. It sticks into a satisfying S bend.

'See it's cooked. Strain the rest through a colander – let's get on.'

The room fills with meaty, saucy smells. The boiling pans of water steam up the windows.

It's time for their cooked spaghetti test.

'Miss, the water's so hot. I can't get it out.'

Bert sucks his scalded fingers.

'Use a fork, spoon, anything but your fingers, Bert. Boiling water scalds.'

Strands of pasta fly to hit the nearest vertical surface and soon my walls and ovens are coated in snakes of spaghetti while the stiff uncooked stuff falls behind cupboards and scatters over the floor. This may be fun but my spaghetti test is turning my classroom into a modern artwork.

We're ready to serve. Twirls of spaghetti onto a take home dish, topped with a mound of sauce and sprinkled with grated Cheddar cheese. It's always Cheddar cheese. Parmesan is off the shopping list as it's another exotic ingredient that could send the meal dogwards, and anyway, we can't afford it.

They bring their dishes for a mark out of ten to reflect effort and more importantly, how much washing up is left in the sink. Then it's covered with foil and put into baskets for collection at home time.

Except for the boys. Boys don't bring baskets or cookery stuff to school. Boys rarely take their cooking home. If I want them to cook then I'll need to shop and they'll pay me back.

'Can we eat it now? We'll clear up, honest.' It's Bert and I'm wary.

So while other teachers gossip, snack and smoke in the staffroom, Bert and his mates transform my cookery room into an eatery. Tables are set with blue seersucker tablecloths, green Beryl Ware plates, forks and spoons, water jugs and glasses. This is a proper sit down meal. It wasn't allowed in my last school, but I'm in charge here and yes, we'll do it properly.

'Let me show you how the Italians eat spaghetti. Don't cut it – Italians think that's rude.'

I twirl my fork round the great long strands and slurp it into my mouth.

'This foreign food's alright Miss. I might cook it tonight.'

Bert and friends clear away and charge out the room as the bell goes for my next lesson.

The queue is jostling outside waiting to make rock cakes and jam buns.

London 1970s

London in the seventies buzzes with energy and there's a frenzy of things to do – wine bars, cheap eating places, art galleries, new musicals and so many theatres. Friends who've arrived in the city have found plenty of job choices, bargain priced flats and they are ready to party. For the past few weeks I've been sharing a flat with Mark, my boyfriend. It's a secret from both sets of parents who might not approve of such goings on before marriage as it is known as living in sin. We're not telling them so they won't know.

My new job as head of home economics is working in a bustling east London comprehensive. Each teaching day I speed out of Hampstead in my ancient Mini Traveller past the halal butchers, Cypriot groceries and Afro Caribbean vegetable stalls and into the suburbs. My new school is in a residential area surrounded by neat streets of Victorian and 1930s terraced houses occupied by white, British working class families who have lived in the area for several generations. Mothers, fathers, aunts and uncles of my students have been to this school, and not much has changed since. The huge factory making ping pong balls and plastic goods is a major employer and many men journey to the east end of London for well paid jobs in the docks and print works. Local shops stock traditional British foods and the early evening hot meal of meat and two veg or a Fray Bentos steak and kidney pie sums it up. I must tread softly and not bring too many of my fancy modern ideas crashing into the classroom.

The real culture shock is what I have to teach. To get them through their cookery exam my teenagers must learn how to make a vast range of high fat, high sugar recipes – pastries, biscuits, cakes and sauces. We'll use as much margarine and lard as I can keep in my gas-fired fridge, and as many packets of Tate and Lyle sugar that can be piled into my food storeroom. Bugger healthy eating. I have to teach them traditional British food. FOR THE EXAM. They must learn that mint sauce is served with roast lamb, horseradish sauce goes with roast beef, and apple sauce with roast pork. These questions are asked in the EXAM and they must learn the RULES.

The cookery textbooks and exam questions pay no attention to multicultural Britain, with little opportunity to celebrate Caribbean cooking and make spicy chicken with fried plantain. No need to learn how to cook dhal or boil a pot of rice. Stir-fried vegetables with noodles and plenty of soya sauce – blah. Falafel with tahini in pitta bread – for goodness sake who would want to eat that. And as for pizza – ridiculous Italian food.

The textbooks tell us daft things such as 'a vegetarian diet has a limited choice and can be bulky and unattractive.' We make junket for sick people for our invalid cookery lesson and there is no mention that some religious groups don't eat foods like bacon, pork pies and sausages.

Things need to change.

Pink nylon overalls

My work uniform is a pale pink nylon overall which just skims the hems of my mini dresses and produces static charge if I'm wearing a crimplene frock underneath. One sleeve hides an armful of elastic bands, essential for scraping back the fashionably long hair of both boys and girls and leads to a few shouty rants.

'My hair's clean and that elastic'll give me split ends.'

The inside skin on the other forearm shows biro notes to remind me of important tasks for the day like 'Check car tyres' or 'Write a letter to Grandma.'

On rare visits to the staffroom, I must remember to remove my overall and rubber gloves before I collapse exhausted into one of the beaten-up staffroom armchairs, and light a cigarette. If not I might be mistaken for the school cleaner and may be told to wash up the coffee cups.

Before we start any cooking, they must obey my chant.

'Hair, hearings and hands – tie your hair back, and remove all jewellery except wedding rings. No-one is married, including me, so bring me your precious things to lock up.'

When my classes find out I'm single, I hear a collective 'Ah'. Prying into the private life of young teachers is a popular diversion in most lessons.

'Have you got a boyfriend, Miss?'

Carol loves gossip – it's a happy time waster. Carol and Vicky wander around school as a pair, and I wonder how I'm going to get them to do any work.

'Carol, it's none of your business – aprons on please.'

'Will you make your own wedding cake? There are cake tins in the cupboard.'

Carol persists in digging for clues.

'Class, and that includes you, Carol, let's see your hands.'

They hold them out for inspection.

'Vicky – take off the nail varnish – the remover's in my desk drawer.'

Vicky tuts with disgust. She'll pay me back for making this fuss. Vicky wants to cook and I'm stopping her with my stupid rules.

The class is checked so we can begin. Once they know I mean business, we speed through the hair, hearings and hands eager to get on with making something to eat.

The TV cooks of the day never obey my hygiene rules. That fancy Fanny Cradock sparkles in her diamond necklace and dangly earrings and even wears an evening dress to cook in. She pokes long red fingernails into pastries and pies and I cringe at the thought of spitting out slivers of red varnish if I ever have to taste her cooking.

One morning, Jim the caretaker is taking down the Housecraft sign on the outside door of my cookery room.

'Jenny. The head wants a new name on your door. What are you called now? Let me know and I'll get a sign made up.'

So am I the Cookery, Home Economics, Domestic Science, Housecraft, Food and Nutrition or Baking teacher?

I wonder if any other teachers have been asked to rename their subject doors. Chemistry could be Blowing things up, Biology – Cutting things up, Woodwork – Sawing things up, History – Old stuff, Art – Colouring stuff, Physics – Boring stuff.

Why do I work in a subject with at least five different names? If a magazine changed its title this often it would have gone bust, out of print and defunct long ago. And it feels as if the future of food teaching is equally dodgy and undervalued.

It doesn't help that the cookery exams in the seventies have different titles. In the sixth form of my high school I begged to study Domestic Science. Sadly the subject was not accepted as an A level for university entrance and I had to take three other A levels as well. My headmistress said I'd never get work if I learnt about cookery. How wrong she was.

Now in this comprehensive school, I have to teach two types of exams – O level for the cleverer ones and CSE for the rest, which is the majority of my classes. And they've got different names too. Cookery, Domestic Science, Home Economics, Housecraft .... Bah.

But for the start of my new job I've got to be fast off the starting block to keep classroom order and my first tactic is to tell everyone that they're doing the EXAM. This is a daft decision, as my end of year results are judged on exam passes and rely upon students turning up for lessons. This is a Senior High School and their last chance to get any qualifications before many of them leave education for good, so exams are important.

But back to my door name. What is it? I am teaching them how to cook.

So let's make a sign called Home Economics. Bah.

Boys don't cook

A gang of grumbly boys bursts into my room. It's an explosive end to my week.

'I ain't doing this lesson. I chose Art. This lesson's for girls or poofters.'

'I'm only here 'cos Mr Smith won't have us in metalwork.'

They glance me up then down, starting with my red platform shoes and up over my beige tights. The school insists that women teachers wear tights or stockings at all times – no bare legs or trousers. Up past my tartan miniskirt and red ribbed top which today feels a bit tight. I'm glad I put on my proper makeup. Plenty of mascara and a swish of purple eyeshadow with shiny baby pink lipstick. Boys, I'm ready for you.

We make fierce eye contact.

'Your names please boys?'

'Gavin!' A burly young giant towers over me.

'Ray!' A shorter, but no less submissive boy scowls back.

'Tim.' Tim short for timid? Or timorous? Hardly.

'Len! Not doing exams, Miss. Leaving at Easter. Got a job in me uncle's garage.'

So Len's not bovvered.

'OK boys – I'll see if you can change back. We don't want you doing lessons that you don't like.'

This school was a secondary modern before it was recently renamed a senior high but the ghost of low expectation lingers on. Most students are entered for some sort of exam unless they choose to leave at the end of the Easter term after they turn sixteen. These early leavers dither aimlessly about the corridors, desperate to sidle out of the school gates and bunk off. And quite a few are listed on my registers.

Mr James, the deputy head says he'll pop into the staffroom and ask if the other teachers will take these boys back into their classes. He returns swiftly to tell me no they're full, and anyway, they only teach serious students who are prepared to study. It seems my grumbly gang can't do subjects like Art, Woodwork, Technical Drawing and Metalwork. But they can do Cookery. It's easy. Just spend lessons making jam tarts and cakes. The new teacher will take you. She doesn't know the kicking-out rules practised by other staff.

The next week the gang is back in the queue propping up the wall outside my room.

'OK all of you, come in and gather round my table with your stools.'

My pink nylon overall covers my much-too-short skirt but I've morphed into The Cookery Teacher.

‘As it’s our first cooking lesson we’re using storeroom ingredients – margarine, caster sugar, eggs and self raising flour. And it’s all free for this lesson, but you’ll need to bring in your own ingredients for the next lessons and leave them in my room in your basket.’

A murmur of horror comes from the back row – basket, bring stuff in. What sort of a lesson are we doing?

‘What are we making today Miss?’ A quiet, nervous girl is speaking from the front row.

‘Your name?’

‘Alice.’ She’s sweet enough to wear her navy coloured Alice band that neatly matches her navy school uniform.

‘Miss – I want to do O level Cookery but I’m in this group.’ She could have added ‘of idiots’ or ‘boys’.

‘Alice, We’ll talk about changing groups later.’

‘Class, we’re making fairy cakes today.’

‘What? I said this lesson was for poofters!’

Gavin stands up to shout – his voice is as large as his size.

‘It’s a simple recipe – the same weight of egg and other ingredients. Beat the margarine with the sugar until it’s creamy.’

I bang my wooden spoon on the edge of the mixing bowl and the soft, shiny mixture plops down. Gavin will be good at this.

‘Crack your egg into a cup, beat it with a fork, stir in, sieve the flour and fold in gently. Then spoon it into paper cases in the tart tins.

Gavin booms again out from his stool.

‘When are we doing tarts, Miss?’

He smirks to the group.

‘I’ve never done a tart.’

I really hope Gavin won’t turn up to my pastry lessons where we learn about rubbing in and knocking up.

‘Aprons on, hair tied back, hands washed – let’s get cooking.’

The room busies with weighing and beating then it’s into the cake cases for baking.

'Wash up while the cakes cook.'

The warm fragrance of baking cakes is calming us all down. Even Gavin is quiet. He's sitting on the floor by his oven, watching his raw cake dough rise and turn golden brown.

'Onto cooling racks and ready for marking.'

'Len. One mark off. You've made seven instead of six. And they are different sizes.'

Len scowls. Stupid rules of fairy cake making.

Alice has six perfectly formed, well risen, golden cakes.

'Full marks Alice.'

'Gavin – six out of ten.' 'What? Why?'

'Sink full of washing up, Gavin – do it before you leave.'

'Class, please remember to bring your ingredients for next time – a choice between pineapple upside down cake and spotted dick.'

I wonder which one Gavin will try.

They pile out the room, fairy cakes packed in paper bags. My boy gang laughs through mouthfuls of sponge and splutters out the crumbs. Only a few bowls and spoons are left in Gavin's sink for me to clear up. Next week I really hope Gavin stays away.

Mr Shield, the headmaster has asked to see me after school and talk over how things are going. It will be a two way exchange. In my previous ILEA school (Inner London Education Authority) we provided all the ingredients for students to do their cooking. Now I've got to teach busy exam classes with an annual food budget of £50. How will I manage? Do I pay for my own demonstrations as well as their tasting sessions for milk and cheese? What happens when students don't bring ingredients in? Can I shop and they pay? I can see some challenges ahead but first I'm going to ask the Science department who pays for the chemicals for their experiments and the Art department if students have to buy art paper and paints when they do a painting and if the games department expects them to bring in their own footballs. Blast it! This is not going to be easy.

She Who Ran Away

Before this new job starts in September I visit my school in my summer holidays to check that everything is shipshape and tidy. The clean, shiny school corridors smell of polish and there's an air of excitement for fresh, new beginnings after the summer break.

Jim, the caretaker, unlocks my door.

Whew. The recent hot, humid weather may account for the stifling heat inside the room but not the smell. Something somewhere is dead or rotting and we need to find it. Twelve cookers line the sides of the room and the hobs are congealed with dark brown sticky spills and lumps of dried food. What was the last teacher cooking and where has she or he gone? No farewell 'Hello and good luck' note. The cooker behind my desk that is used for demonstrations shows evidence of a massive fry up. Blobs of beige grease hang from the eye level grill and drip onto burnt bits in the frying pan below. As I open the oven door, it's clear this cooker has gone through a baking marathon. Even the glass door is splattered with a thick brown layer of entrenched fat.

'Jim, when do these ovens get cleaned up before I start?'

My arm sweeps around to the other cookers which are as filthy as ones left in a student squat.

He looks sheepish, opens the windows to let the air in or out and heads for the door. I wonder if he thinks I'm too young to be head of department at twenty three years old, in charge of the mighty task of running two cookery rooms and a school flat.

'The teacher has to do it. I'll let you get on – just put a note under my door when you leave.'

'But Jim – who taught here last and why did she or he go...?'

Too late – he's disappeared into his sparkling corridors and down to the caretaker's hideaway.

From now on let's call her SHE WHO RAN AWAY. And add AND LEFT ME WITH THIS SH*T.

But onto tracing the smell – I can't have classes arriving to this putrid stink.

Imagine the 'Ugh, Miss, vile smell' comments or 'I ain't staying in this.' They'll be out before I can say 'My name is ...'

A door from inside my room opens into the huge storeroom which could shed some light on the cooking history of this department and maybe hold the clue to the rot. The high ceilinged room is stacked with enough equipment to supply any professional kitchen shop.

What has She Who Ran Away been doing? On the top shelf is a row of long, aluminium fish kettles with lids – big enough to hold some large, unaffordable salmon. So was she cooking for weekend weddings? Jim must bring me a step ladder if we're going to reach those. It will probably be me reaching them. Alone.

Next some flat, black, cast iron griddle pans with welded, curved handles – the sort you see in a stately home kitchen for cooking griddle cakes. Then there are large aluminium preserving pans for jams, marmalades and chutneys.

And sets of tins for a class of twenty or more students. Oblong bread tins, large round Christmas cake tins, Swiss roll and domed sponge flan tins as well as the heavily used and battered Victoria sandwich tins. Piles of beautifully moulded tins to make éclairs, jam tarts, fairy cakes and tiny Yorkshire puddings. Hanging on hooks are metal rings for pastry flans – plain for savoury and fluted for sweet. Do not put your pastry in the wrong ring. Then some pointy tins that look like piping bags, that I reckon are used for cream horns. Was this woman running a private bakery as well?

At floor level there are essential saucepans, frying pans and a collection of pressure cookers, metal colanders and sieves. And stacks of aluminium holey steamers which fit on top of saucepans to steam stuff like jam roly poly and treacle sponges.

She Who Ran Away seems to have taught a marathon of baking dishes and their history can be traced from the encrusted bits of cake, dough and burnt pastry that need to be cleaned off before I can begin.

And if I ask Jim who is going to clean up all this equipment I reckon I'll get a 'The teacher has to do it' answer.

So tomorrow I'll drive back in my Mini Traveller, leaving my friends and Mark lazing on rugs on leafy Hampstead Heath drinking wine and eating picnics with baguettes and Brie. And I'll be sweating in my stinky room ready to begin the filthy task.

The teacher has to do it. But this still doesn't account for the smell.

My early morning drive the next day is hot, very hot and the room still smells of rot. I need to get on. We've got a street party tonight and Mark will bring bottles of wine and I'll make a pile of sausage rolls.

Overall and rubber gloves on, I fill the deep butlers' sinks with scorching hot water and stir in the caustic soda crystals just like my grandmother taught me. The dirty baking trays, cake tins and saucepans are piled on the wooden draining boards ready for soaking. Caustic soda is dangerous stuff, so I need to be careful, but there is a joy in watching burnt bits of food float off from the trays into the scummy water as I leave them to soak.

Now to explore the ingredients in the storeroom and track down the smell. Two large plastic bins contain catering sacks of plain and self raising flour and the shelves are stacked with packs of Tate and Lyle granulated, caster, icing and brown sugar. A row of huge screw top glass jars are filled with bright red glacé cherries, vivid green stems of crystallised angelica, currants, sultanas, raisins, mixed peel, desiccated coconut and almond flakes.

A section of any school food storeroom shelves must be filled with bottles of artificial colouring and flavourings to prop up our culinary skills and enhance 1970s dishes. She Who Run Away has left tiny bottles of red, green and yellow food colouring and essences of vanilla, almond and rum. Red is for rhubarb, pink butter icing and to colour the glaze for strawberry tarts. Green is added to dishes made with gooseberries and cooked apples.

Vanilla essence, in a very large brown bottle, is the most popular chemical compote added to fairy cakes and Victoria sandwich. I mix drops of almond essence with semolina for Bakewell tart instead of ground almonds which are too expensive. Rum essence is the ultimate sin, which we dribble into sponges or chocolate truffles at Christmas time. How I long to use the real thing.

And there are so many ground spices which must be for Christmas baking – cinnamon, ginger, cloves, allspice and whole nutmegs like my grandmother grates on the top of her rice puddings. I open the ground ginger pot hoping for a whiff of brandy snaps and ginger biscuits but the brown dust has lost its spicy magic long ago.

On the floor there are heavy plastic containers, sticky with black treacle and golden syrup both with drippy lids, some huge catering tins of red jam, peach slices and a massive jar of Heinz Salad cream. On the shelf above is a row of small tins of Carnation condensed milk. Was she running a sweet factory making toffee and fudge? What the hell was going on in this kitchen?

A cardboard tray of eggs gently warms in the summer heat in a corner of the storeroom. How old are they? Are they safe to use? I'll have to do the jug of water test and see if they float. Bob to the top and they're in the bin along with the old pots of spices.

That only leaves the fridge behind my desk. This strange, gas-powered contraption rumbles away, working overtime to manage its cooling job in the August heat. Surely it will have been emptied before the start of the summer holidays? But no. On the top shelf a metal jug has a pastry brush stuck rigidly in some yellowy brown glob. Looks like her egg glaze pot. Maybe she made some savoury stuff like sausage rolls, cheese straws or Cornish pasties? The shelves below are packed with blocks of lard and a large plastic tub labelled Catering Margarine which smells of fish oil and is flecked with crumbs and smears of jam.

It's time to put the kettle on and test the Typhoo tea bags and dried milk left in the storeroom. And a cup full of glacé cherries, angelica, sultanas and almonds as my lunchtime snack. No time to go down to the bakery at the end of the road – I need to get on and throw stuff away.

The afternoon passes quickly scrubbing the mountain of cookware that emerges stripped clean from the caustic bath. Eclair and jam tart tins are really beautiful kitchen pieces, fit for an antique shop, and will last us for many more years. As I brush the pastry bits from the cream horn tins, I secretly wish that She Who Ran Away would come back and share her cooking legacy or at least give me her recipes and tell me what she was making. She may have left a pile of *Cooking is Fun* books, but a real life pastry cook could teach me a lot of things I don't know and have never made.

The smell of putrefying something or other is still there, but it's time to drive back to the fun and party time in Hampstead.

The next day it's a later start. Our street party lasted well into the early morning and both Mark and myself are nursing headaches.

Today's job is to label and sort the drawers and cupboards under the students' worktables. I'm making them responsible for their own stuff and each drawer is lined with brown paper and drawn with equipment outlines. At the end of each lesson I'll march round and check – it's like the card game Memory. If anything is missing they must search the sinks and bins and no-one leaves till all the equipment is accounted for. I can't have cook's knives hidden in duffle bags or dirty pans left in the sinks.

But still where's that rotting smell coming from? A sniff test round my room leads to my desk. I call Jim and ask him to unlock the drawer and please, leave the key behind. Inside are the putrid remains of an unidentifiable sandwich. She Who Ran Away must have gone off in a real hurry if she left her lunch behind. But there are other unattractive smells.

'Jim, can you help me pull out the cupboards from the wall please? I'll make you a cup of tea.'

His look implies that he'd rather be left undisturbed in his caretaker's room quietly making his own brew.

Our furniture shift exposes leftover baking bits, dirty jam tart tins and the skeleton of a dead mouse.

'Please Jim, can the cleaners come and sort this out? Please.'

I'm done – my room is nearly ready for the new term in my new job in my new school and it's the weekend and it's hot. Mark will take me for a trip to the seaside in his posh company car, and we'll eat crab sandwiches on the beach and breathe in the ozone-filled air.

Apple crumble

Making apple crumble is like taking a dance class. Their tables are arranged all around me and I dance about in the middle giving instructions and spot dems. A spot dem means I use their ingredients rather than my own to show the techniques for the recipe. With a £50 food budget for the year, a spot dem saves me spending on ingredients for a dish I don't want to take home.

'Class. We're making apple crumble using the rubbing in method which is a very important skill.'

Gavin must be listening as he raises his large head from his slump on the Formica table.

'Sieve the flour and sugar into your mixing bowl, rub in the margarine till it looks like breadcrumbs then twist and shake the bowl to find lumps.'

I lift Len's floury sugar into the air, let it drop into the bowl and squeeze in chunks of margarine with my fingertips.

'What is this method called?'

'Rubbing in Miss.'

'Thanks Len.'

'Miss, if it's an important skill do we need to practice?'

Gavin sniggers his question. It's a wind-up and I know he's not thinking of cooking. Cookery recipes are littered with rude words and I speed up so the innocents don't catch on and claim my lesson has taught them dirty words.

'Alright, let's get on. Bert lift then squeeze. Don't squash it into a lump.'

Bert likes his food and he's not keen when I do spot dems as I can't give him my demonstration dish as a swap for his help in clearing up.

Flour and sugar dust floats in the air.

'How do we know when it is like breadcrumbs, class?'

They chorus the answer.

'Twist and Shake, Miss.'

'Just like Chubby Checker, class. Twist again like we did last summer.'

Who am I talking about? Some American rock singer that had a big hit in the sixties when they were tiny.

The class lifts their mixing bowls, twists their hips and shakes any lumps of fat to the top. They wait for my approving inspection as I dance around the tables.

'Perfect Janice.' Girls are dainty with cool hands. Boys have clumsy, hot hands which can quickly squeeze the crumble into a fatty ball.

My Twist and Shake routine is used for a myriad of fatty, floury recipes and we must progress through the skills of combining the ingredients FOR THE EXAM – crumble, shortcrust pastry, rock cakes, flaky and rough puff. Deep down I think it's a way of using cheap ingredients to make high fat, sugary cakes and pastries to fill us up. The British diet and cookery lessons will have to change.

Let's get this lesson nailed. They peel, core and slice a cooking apple into a small foil dish, sprinkle with sugar and cinnamon, then top with the light, crumbly crumble which bakes to a golden crunchiness. The room has a spicy fragrance and I wish I had a demonstration dish for my supper.

'We've mastered one of the basic skills. What's the method called?'

'Rubbing in Miss. Does your boyfriend know how to do it?'

Gavin smirks at the answer but most are just pleased to take this tasty pudding home.

Mark

Mark and I met during Freshers' Week at Bristol University. He and his flatmate Sid hatched a get-a-girlfriend plan and invited newly arrived students from my all female hall of residence to tea. It worked for both of them. Meeting Mark was a moment from Mills and Boon – a tall, dark, clever, handsome man with a car. His ancient, convertible baby blue Morris Minor with a red interior trim was a great attraction.

Mark left university a year before me to work in London and I followed after my degree and we linked up again. He's got a job selling wine and spirits around central London pubs – he says it's to get experience before an international job with the company. But for now our evening date can find me perched on a bar stool, ordering his latest drink promotion. The most embarrassing campaign so far is for the French aperitif, Lillet. He has no clue that this is the name of the popular sanitary tampon and I cringe when I have to ask the barman 'Can I have a Lillet, please?'

Eating out and food shopping are our favourite weekend pastimes and London has such diverse communities with street markets to explore. Soho street food stalls spill with new fruit and vegetables – mangoes, avocados and guavas which I'm eager to try. Then on to Lina Stores in Soho, our favourite Italian delicatessen, to stock up on dried and fresh pasta and hunks of Parmesan cheese. The aroma of hams and salamis hanging from the ceiling hooks and the smell of freshly roasted coffee hits you as you open the door. Chinatown for a quick dim sum lunch and a hunt through the busy Chinese grocery shops for hundred year old eggs, rice and dried noodles, soya sauce and big bags of spices. And anything weird that catches my eye. Brixton street market is far out from north London but it's the place to shop for dried salt fish and tins of ackee to surprise our friends with a Jamaican saltfish and ackee supper and buy spicy plantain chips from the street food stalls.

Charlotte Street is our favourite place for a night out, eating food from around the world. Schmidt's German restaurant for schnitzel, goulash and real German cakes, Elena's L'Etoile for its thudding French food and the many Greek Cypriot restaurants selling kebabs wrapped in hot pitta bread. Restaurants are springing up in Camden and Hampstead all the time. The new Pizza Palace claims to cook pizza like the Romans and the Spaghetti House serves the weirdest pasta dishes. We can eat our way around the world within a few miles.

Pickled onions and chutney

Since I'm short of funds for my lessons, I've asked for donations of spare fruits and vegetables for our lessons on preservation. London gardens spill out their windfall apples and pears and we get plenty of beetroot and onions from the pickings of allotments. The keener students bring in blackberries and crab apples gathered in forays around Epping Forest or derelict land near the school.

Now my tables are piled with boxes of apples in various stages of decay and a large sack of small onions donated by the school gardener.

The class shambles in and settles on their stools.

'These lessons are about preserving things so that they will last longer. How are we going to preserve these apples and onions so that they keep over winter?'

Silence. They don't care.

'Come on, what shall we do with them?'

'Put them on the compost heap, Miss – them apples look rotten.'

Bert is good in the school garden so he should know. And he's right – we need to remove the battered and bruised fruit but I must teach thriftiness in this throwaway world.

'We're going to use the apples to make apple chutney and pickle those small onions in vinegar.'

From the grumbles and shuffling they'd rather repeat last week's fairy cakes lesson.

'Hurry up – you have to make a choice. Apple chutney or pickled onions?'

They divide by sex. Girls choose chutney, boys the onions. This separation often happens. They are not choosing what they want to cook. The boys and girls just don't want to work with each other.

On a school training day we're told to mix up boys and girls, make them sit next to each other and work in mixed sex pairs.

One evening Mark drove me past the deer in Richmond Park. 'An outing to look at the rutting.' he teases. The female deer huddle together and the giant stags, pumped high with testosterone, roar and patrol their boundaries. No one makes them mix up. I think Mark must have plans for us later.

In the classroom, while the girls cook in clean, organised workplaces, the boys create a messy nest of ingredients which soon spill onto the floor and end up being kicked under the tables.

Large teenage boys preparing tiny onions make me laugh as they peel away the withered, brown skins, then top and tail the onions and put them into salted water. Gradually the tears flow.

'What's up Bert? Does this lesson make you sad?'

Bert rubs his fists into his eyes. Now his whole face is pink and blubbery.

'Class – don't wipe your eyes with oniony hands – the juice gets in and makes the crying worse.' They blink, reddened and bleary.

'Me Nan peels her onions under water.' It's Len who tells me that he lives with his Nan and they each help prepare their evening tea. He says my lessons are his favourite, and I can see how Nan has shared her cooking skills. As he dumps his onions in a bowl of cold water, a stream of dribble runs from his nose, over his chin and splashes in. Plop! Pickled onions and snot – now how are we going to make that safe to eat?

Squeals come from Carol and Vicky who are peeling and chopping some windfall apples.

Carol pins a slug with the tip of her paring knife and its innards ooze onto the table. They group in disgust to watch the slug shrivel in green slime.

'Err Miss – look at this slug – I ain't using them apples.'

Carol holds the dying slug up for the boys to share her revulsion.

'OK, girls. Throw the bruised bits of apples away. We're still going to use the rest.'

'Miss, I ain't eating things with slugs in. Why do I have to do this lesson anyway?'

Carol unties her apron, slings it on the table, heads for the door and beckons Vicky to follow. This is Carol's usual trick to meet her boyfriend at the school gates, but her boyfriend might not find the smell of vinegar and rotting fruit so attractive today. Carol tells me that school, and my lessons in particular, are rubbish. Vicky just trots behind her nodding in agreement.

The remaining girls stir the compote of apples, onions, vinegar and brown sugar into a bubbling broth.

The boys pack their tiny onions into warm Kilner jars and pour in hot Sarson's malt vinegar.

The fragrance from my room often attracts wandering staff and students who sniff the air and open the door and go 'Ah! Bisto!' like the TV ad. Biff is a frequent visitor. He gets sent out of lessons to drift around the school in search of mischief and sources of entertainment.

'Miss – this room always smells lovely – when can I do cooking with you? Please let me in.'

'One day Biff – maybe. Now get on your way. I expect the head is waiting to see you.' I hope it's not for him to be caned.

Steaming apple chutney is piled into jam jars, covered with waxed paper, topped with cellophane and sealed with an elastic band.

The labels on the jars are designed for the highest marks.

Alice's Amazing Apple Chutney 1972.

Paul's Perfect Pickled Onions.

Maybe some are still maturing in a secret east London cupboard, waiting for discovery. And maybe, like Lea and Perrins Worcestershire sauce, they will become a mass produced delicacy found on future supermarket shelves.

Discipline matters

When they interviewed me for the job of running this department the first question was 'Can you keep your classes in order?'

I answered firmly that I'd survived for two years in an ILEA comprehensive school and I was confident that I'd cope. Now I've got my doubts. There have been some very shouty lessons since I started, and days when they've barged out the room leaving sinks full of dirty washing up. If I can't keep order, I can't do this job. It's as simple as that.

But who can help? During our PGCE studies at London University no one tackles the serious issue of how to manage boisterous teenagers and get them to learn. As I walk around the school, I hear some loud voices, see naughty students leaning on walls outside classrooms, but then pass quiet, busy classrooms where the students clearly treat the lessons with respect.

Mr Lewes is the man for advice and I trust him to keep my secret. He's taught at the school for years and students pass him in the corridors with a polite 'Hello, Mr Lewes.' He knows the families of the students and has taught some of them too. I bet he never dreads some classes as I do. How does he do it? Am I too young and too new? What techniques must I use? How I'd love to hear a 'Good morning, Miss Hyde' instead of 'Look at her – is she new?'

'Jenny, you'll be fine. Make them know you mean business. Plan your lessons carefully and don't let them get away with things.'

'But I want to be like you. I want to walk into any class and get their attention. My classes are really noisy and excitable.'

'Jenny, we're all different, and teachers have their own ways of running successful classrooms. You're strong and determined, so I know you'll succeed.'

We come up with a plan. My classes already line up outside my room and I let them in when quiet. But once inside there's often a tussle and a few thumps between the boys. Mr Lewes says he'll deal with the ones who regularly forget their homework, cooking ingredients or money to pay for stuff and until things settle, they cannot eat at lunchtime in my room. And there will be no mention of the cane.

Now I've got a theory about them eating in my room. We fuss about laying the table and using proper plates, then we sit down together. And talk and share. And sometimes they tell me about their families. And sometimes they share unfair things. They get a 'Mind your own business' if they ask for any of my secrets, but I'm pleased to chat and enjoy their teenage banter.

Mr Lewes is insistent. 'Lock your room at break times, visit the staffroom and mix with the other teachers. And come and join us at the pub on Friday evenings.'

This sounds like a very grown up agreement but the pub down the road does not fill me with glee. It's a dismal, 1930s building designed for smoking, drinking and old men. During opening hours the Public Bar is filled with a lot of them. I'd rather be with my jolly friends in the pubs of Hampstead sipping cold lager and eating crisps.

Going metric

In the 1970s school cookery rooms around Britain received instructions to replace all cooking equipment that uses old imperial measures like pounds, ounces, pints and inches. WE ARE GOING METRIC.

Out go sturdy metal jugs to measure pints and fluid ounces and in come plastic ones with metric millilitres.

Out go the heavy weighing scales with metal weights in pounds and ounces. In comes cheap, plastic scales measuring grams and kilos. They have a plastic arm that swings round a dial, and when boys push too hard on the weighing bowl, the arm snaps off, broken forever.

Our money went metric on February 15th 1971 and how people moaned that it was a trick to put up prices. The five new pence coins replaced the shilling, and we use fifty new pence coins instead of ten shilling notes. Adding up metric money is easy. Changing my school recipes into grams and litres is a real headache. The maths is complicated. There are 28.35 grams to the ounce, 453.6 grams to the pound, one pint is 568.2 millilitres, and one inch is 2.54 centimetres. People round numbers up or down and no clear guidance arrives for swapping from imperial into metric.

Outside the classroom the world carries on with the old measurements. Milkmen deliver milk in pint glass bottles, pubs sell pints of beer and the greengrocer prices his fruit and vegetables in old money and weighs them by the pound. Shops sell packets of lard and margarine in half pounds and flour in three pound paper bags. BUT I HAVE TO GO METRIC IN MY CLASSROOM.

All my handwritten school recipes are in metric and on days when they cook their favourite recipe from home, it leads to chaos. They bring in treasured cuttings from magazines and newspapers and even Nan's handwritten recipe book. Liz is stern with me.

'Nan says you need to use pounds and ounces to cook this cake else it won't work.'

I wonder if, in the future, someone will have to look up what oz, lb and pt mean.

The Governor's tea

Dawn, the school secretary, pops her head round my cookery room door.

'Jenny, can you make the Governor's tea next week? Oh, and by the way, the head says he will increase the capitation for your ingredients but please provide evidence to show how much money you need for the year.'

This kind woman has nurtured me since I arrived and it's no time to complain about extra work.

'Normally about fifteen to twenty people turn up. Nothing fancy. We just need a few sandwiches and some scones, biscuits and homemade cakes. The teacher before you got the girls to do it. We'll pay you for the ingredients.'

Well, that's alright then. The girls can do it. On top of all the other things they are learning and cooking in my lessons, somehow me and the girls will find time to prepare a not-too-fancy homemade tea for fifteen to twenty people.

I wonder if visitors to my cookery room have any idea of what it takes to manage my large classes who cook throughout the day. My door bursts open first thing as students bring baskets of ingredients for lessons. Then deliveries arrive from the butcher or greengrocer. I'm emptying the dryer and folding clean tea towels and dishcloths, hanging up clean aprons and shoving those that need repair into a drawer.

Next to register my form group, then classes stream in ready to cook, eat, clear and pack, get homework, find out what to bring next week or come for help with revision. When the bell rings at the end of school, I tidy my food storeroom, check the eight sinks, twelve cookers, cupboards full of mucky baking tins, saucepans, frying pans, drawers full of cooking tools, and my precious, locked cupboard holding a few old electrical whisks and a Kenwood Chef. I wash dishcloths and tea towels again in the ancient twin tub, spin them just damp and hang them back in the gas-fired dryers ready for the morning when they must be folded and packed away again. Then sweep and clean the room before the cleaners turn up – they won't do it if it's too messy. I check that the ovens and gas rings are turned off, and that the rubbish is ready for collection.

'Bye' teachers call as they scurry past my room, off to the pub or home to a cosy family and a cooked dinner.

Much later I collect my marking and list the food to buy for the next day. And all with no help.

In my first week, a lad brings over a pile of muddy football shirts, socks and shorts.

'Sir says can you wash and dry these? The last teacher did it.'

Of course, I will find time to prepare the Governor's tea and wash the bloody football shirts. I'm new here and want to get on with people, but somehow, sometime things must change. Unless they'd like me to sleep in the school flat.

On my drive back to Hampstead I plan my argument.

In this school, does the Art department paint the school walls?

Do English students write the school brochures?

Will Maths present the school accounts?

And does Science manage the school grounds and dig the gardens as part of their biology studies? No.

SO WHY SHOULD I PREPARE A LITTLE GOVERNOR'S TEA FOR UP TO 20 PEOPLE AND WASH THE BLOODY FOOTBALL KIT.

My grandmother told me that one good turn deserves another. And it is my turn.

Carol and Vicky are a natural choice for the tea task. This pair of school scallywags never bring ingredients to my lessons, and instead sprawl heads down on the worktables, comparing their latest boyfriends, picking their split ends and flicking bits onto my floor. They've cooked their way through the cheap ingredients in my storeroom and are bored with making jam tarts and scones. Any reprimand from me gets a tornado reply.

'Miss, we're leaving at Easter, you can't make us do nothing.'

Other teachers have somehow removed them from their registers and it seems this pair is mine, for whole afternoons until they leave school.

'Carol and Vicky – you're going to make the Governor's tea. Here are the recipes, write a shopping list to buy the food next week. This is the menu.'

I pass them a handwritten list:

Governor's tea menu
Egg and salad cream sandwiches
Asparagus rolls with brown bread and butter
Fruit scones with butter twirls
Brandy snaps with whipped cream
Butterfly cakes with piped butter icing
Tea with milk and sugar

When I worked as a waitress in Wicksteed Park's Tea Pavilion in Kettering these are things we'd serve for afternoon tea. The Park is famous for its crunchy brandy snaps which we serve with a swirl of piped cream. Brandy snaps look impressive but are really hard to make and I hope that Carol and Vicky are up to the challenge.

The day before the tea party Carol and Vicky grumble in with shopping baskets laden with golden syrup, Heinz salad cream, boxes of eggs, punnets of mustard and cress and show-off cans of asparagus. My elaborate Governor's tea menu is a cunning plan to increase my food stocks. After this first baking session, we'll have plenty of spare ingredients and I can use real butter instead of that catering pack of County Supply Margarine that tastes of fish.

On tea party day the rest of the class busies themselves making Swiss roll. Carol and Vicky must dress to impress as someone might pop in to check the tea progress, and they won't want to see a scruffy pair messing with their food.

'Girls, hang up your duffle coats, take out your chewing gum, tie back your hair, and wash your hands. Then put on clean overalls before you start.'

Ha ha! I've got a couple of white cook's overalls ready for special occasions. As they button up, the girls transform. Their short skirts and half undone ties are hidden. A pair of smart cooks emerges.

I've prepared the hostess trolley with tray cloths, teapots, milk jugs, sugar bowls, teacups and saucers, small plates and serving platters. We need napkins and knives, cake forks and teaspoons, tablecloths and d'oyleys. And we mustn't forget the tea strainer. We're serving proper tea and need to make sure that all the china and cutlery is sparkling.

'Carol and Vicky, can you check that everything is clean?'

They glower at me.

'Why can't someone else do this, Miss?'

'Because they want to do an EXAM and you don't.'

This tea will test their stamina. As they start their baking marathon I keep a watchful eye knowing that at any time they could erupt, slam down their tools and leave the room shouting 'We ain't doing no more. We ain't your cooking slaves.'

Into the oven go the scones, then a swift clear up ready for the sponges which they will transform into butterfly cakes. Finally our biggest cooking challenge of all – brandy snaps.

Dollops of gingery, sugary, syrupy dough go into the hottest oven and out come golden brown craters which must be worked at speed. Each snap is lifted, wrapped round a wooden spoon handle and held in place till it forms a roll. Your hands feel warm and greasy, but there is no time to enjoy this pleasure. There are trayfuls to process and more baking in the oven.

I join team Carol and Vicky to finish off the brandy snaps with piped cream, glacé cherries and tiny angelica leaves. Wicksteed Park would be proud.

Then it's on with the sandwiches.

Peeled, hard boiled eggs, mashed smooth with salad cream, mixed with mustard and cress then spread onto soft Mother's Pride white bread with the crusts removed and cut into quarters.

We drain precious mushy spears of asparagus from the cans and place them on buttered brown bread, roll them tightly and cut into small portions. Canned asparagus is expensive and portions cannot be too generous.

The sandwiches go on a plate with a plain d'oyley. D'oyleys matter in my cookery world. Plain for savoury, frilly for sweet, and these rules must not be broken.

Another hostess trolley is piled with sandwiches, buttered fruit scones, brandy snaps, and butterfly cakes.

The rest of the class gathers to coo over Carol and Vicky's work, amazed that these two can produce anything edible. The feast is finished with hot brewed tea and we wheel the trolleys into the headmaster's study. The Governors smile but I'm more thrilled at the surprised looks from the teachers on the school panel who know this unruly pair from their wanderings around the school corridors.

Carol and Vicky return with me to my cookery room. I'm too tired to ask them to clear up. Instead I give them a bag of spare sandwiches and cakes.

'Thanks girls – you've been great. Impressive cooking. Oh and have you got my shopping change?'

Vicky offers me a handful of coins then they throw down their overalls and resume their usual scruffiness as they wander off into the dark night, cackling through mouthfuls of sandwich.

The next morning I arrive early as usual, to start a busy day. In despair, I see the hostess trolleys, parked outside my room, piled with dirty teacups, empty plates, crumpled napkins and teapots full of cold tea leaves. As my form group catches up on their gossip, I don my overall and rubber gloves to clear up before my cooking classes arrive.

That weekend I prepare my case for Mr Shield, the head and chief fund donor. I need ancillary help and more money for ingredients. This cannot go on. I won't teach, clean up and be a drudge on my own.

A few days later, I get a note telling me to come after school and interview candidates for the ancillary position. Help is coming.

The following week, my chosen angel, the marvellous Cynthia, will arrive to be my right hand woman and saviour and work with me for five hours a week. It's not enough, but it's a start.

The school secretary pops her head round the door with more news.

'Jenny, you'll be pleased to know the school kitchens have agreed to take over making the Governor's teas.'

As my grandmother said, one turn deserves another.

I hear later that the PE department is buying an automatic washing machine and tumble dryer, and I am free to soar ahead and teach my subject with no distractions.

Rock cakes

My mother is an expert rock cake cook and can turn the plain mixture into jam buns and a horrid seed cake by adding black, spiky caraway seeds that look like mouse droppings and taste of medicine.

My sister took a biscuit tin full of our mother's rock cakes on her travels with her boyfriend by Land Rover to Tehran. At the Turkish-Iran border she used them as bribes when stopped for papers and permits. She's blond and looks like Farrah Fawcett Major so she was lucky that the border guards were only interested in her buns and not her body. And lucky they didn't search the Land Rover's dashboard compartment and find the gun that her boyfriend had hidden.

Rock cakes are a middle range cooking skill, lodged between apple crumble and shortcrust pastry.

My teaching practice tutor said that shifting from easy to challenging recipes was Progression, but when I see sticky, fatty fingers squeezing a soggy flour dough it's more like a Mess.

By now they know the rules for rubbing in.

'Come on Ray – show how it's done.'

He wobbles his hips and joggles his mixing bowl, picks the lumps and squeezes.

'Add your sultanas and mixed peel and stir to a soft dough with eggy milk.'

The contents of my sultana jar have shrunk and I wonder which boys have sneaked into the storeroom and scooped them out for snacks.

'Put little piles on your greased baking tray, Ray.'

'Piles Miss? How big is a pile?'

Ray twizzles to the class and he's on the tease.

'OK, put spoonfuls on the tray then into the oven for 20 minutes.'

There are warm, spicy smells as I circle the room, crouching to look into the ovens to see if the cakes are turning brown. A nod when they're ready. I reckon some boys ask for extra checks just to get a glimpse of my underwear. Oh for the day when we can wear trousers, like the men.

It's marking time and Ray protests when I tell him that his cakes are too hard and slightly burnt.

'Miss... please. If they are called rock cakes, they should be like rocks. Mine are brown rocks. Give me a better mark.'

Cynthia

Before the end of Friday school, Cynthia, my new helper pops in to see what she needs for her new job on Monday. Cynthia will help with cleaning, washing and organising the food ingredients.

'Hello Miss Hyde.'

As she enters the room she gives a nod to some of the boys.

'Hello again, Cynthia. I'm very pleased to see you and do call me Jenny.'

I hear whispers of 'Jenny, Jenny. Her name is Jenny.'

Learning a new teacher's first name is the second most valuable secret. Teachers are always called by their surnames. Mr Smith, Mrs Bates.... and the sad Miss So-and-so's who are destined for a solitary life in a rented room, spending their evenings at home with their cat, marking school work. Somehow we teachers are not like other humans and the discovery that we have a first name is met with shock and giggles.

'Mr Smith's name is Albert, and I heard someone call Mrs Bates Deirdre.' OOOh, fancy that.

I imagine they gather in corners, passing recently found names to the Chief Name Collector who holds the First Name List for Teachers and shouts to the crowd of adoring followers.

'I've just got that new one. The baking teacher. She's called Jenny.'

And they bow down to the Chief Name Collector in awe and wonder.

The first and most highly prized secret is finding out about the teacher's private life. Married teachers can be boring with their husbands, wives and children. Well, boring until they start an affair with someone in the staffroom. There are some teachers, at the top of the school hierarchy, whose first names I never know like the head, deputy head and my discipline saviour, Mr Lewes.

When new teachers arrive in school, the gossip scavengers are out in force. Male teachers are just called Mr and don't attract as much interest as the women, who are addressed as Miss if they are single, so it's Miss Hyde for me and they're after my first name and secrets on my private life.

'Have you got a boyfriend, Miss? What's his name? Where do you live? Where does he live? Will we meet him if he comes to collect you from school? Are you getting married?'

If you tell them 'No' and 'None of your business', then they persist.

'Why not, Miss? You're not that old.'

It is comforting that at twenty three they think I still stand a chance of married life. Like the grubbiest of reporters from the *News of the World*, they are constantly on my case, checking for updates. I privately hope that with Cynthia's help, I'll have more of a social life and give these gossip mongers some fuel.

Back in the cookery room, the class is packing away their rock cakes, ready for home time.

'Would you like a cup of tea, Cynthia?'

'I can see you are busy, Jenny. Let me make us one.'

Incredible. Amazing. Kindness, support and a cuppa are coming. My simple prayers have been answered. The first term in this new school has been difficult. Firstly I have to make sure that I'm teaching them interesting, relevant, up to date stuff on food and nutrition to get them through the EXAMS. Next is keeping order in the classroom. Then finally, it's managing the food and ingredients that arrive daily in my room, cleaning the ovens, equipment, and washing tea towels, dishcloths and aprons.

Now, after all this time running things on my own, Cynthia is here. The marvellous, energetic, nothing-is-too-much-trouble, laughing Cynthia.

As the students begin to leave, Cynthia helps them pack up their cooking and sees a dirty baking tray lurking in a butler's sink.

'Do you want Len and his friend to clear this up, Jenny? I think they must have forgotten.'

Len glances at Cynthia and returns to the sink to complete his washing up. As soon as the room is empty we sit down, and as I unbutton my overall and crumple it onto a stool, I feel my responsibilities peel away.

Cynthia is here. Help is at hand.

'Cynthia, you seem to know some of the boys, like Len.'

'Oh, Jenny, I know lots of them. They've probably been round my house for tea. One of my children is at this school, and me girl is coming next year. We've lived round here for years. Me mother and father moved here from the east end. They're nice kids in this area. You won't get any stick from them. Any trouble, then just have a word with their parents. But I really came to ask what would you like me to bring to wear for this job.'

She glances at my tired, discarded overall.

'I think an apron and some rubber gloves will be fine.'

Before leaving, Cynthia washes and puts away our teacups. I shake her hand warmly.

My weekend stretches ahead and a walk on Hampstead Heath in the autumn sunshine with Mark will be perfect. Then back to our cosy flat for roast dinner.

Cynthia is coming on Monday, and I won't be alone.

Angel Delight

I'm really in love with Angel Delight, especially the butterscotch flavour. What a magical new product this is. Add milk to the powder, then whisk until it thickens to peaks of buttery, sugary, foamy chemical alchemy. It's finger lickingly good. But what is it made from? There are no clues on the packet but why should I care?

I send my mother a coupon for a free packet explaining that it takes less than a minute to make. She's a busy primary school headmistress, and Angel Delight could be her answer for speedy puds. I get no thankyou's in her letters back to me and I wonder if she'd say 'it's muck' like she did when I tossed her lettuce, picked fresh from her garden, in French dressing instead of using salad cream.

Today we're making Angel Delight tart for our lesson on Convenience Foods. The class brings in a packet with their choice of flavour – vanilla, chocolate, strawberry and the perfectly scrumptious butterscotch. I've bought some ready baked pastry shells that we'll fill with Angel Delight and sprinkle Hundreds and Thousands on the top. Another new product that comes in loads of bright colours and gives a crunchy, sugary topping to this amazing dish. My mother would be horrified.

Staff have collected empty packets and cans that they use at home and left them in my room. My demonstration table is laden with colourful display boxes of Instant Whip, Bird's Chocolate Blancmange powder, a can of Campbell's Condensed Mushroom Soup, Green's Sponge Mix, and a packet of Quick Jel. Then there's the essential convenience stuff from my storeroom – Carnation Evaporated Milk and bottles of Heinz Salad Cream and Tomato Ketchup.

I hold up the cardboard carton of Vesta Beef Curry that Mrs Smith said was her favourite. It still has a whiff of exotic spices.

'Class,this lesson's all about using convenience foods to make our lives easier. Mrs Smith says this curry's so quick – just add hot water and it's ready.'

Bert puts his hand up as the rest gather on the stools.

'Miss, me mum says you're supposed to teach us cooking, not opening packets.'

Len mumbles something about not eating foreign food.

'Look. We have to learn about convenience foods for the exam. Angel Delight tart is a perfect convenience food for easy puddings for busy mothers. It saves lots of bother.'

My brain cells scream at the nonsense coming out of my mouth. There is no food yet invented that looks remotely like the creamy, soft foam of butterscotch Angel Delight. It is not a convenient way of inventing anything, just a spectacular triumph on its own. Does it really need to be mixed with milk? Will water do instead or is this part of the Drinka Pinta Milka Day campaign?

I show them how to whip the powder and milk into foamy peaks, then I pile the Angel Delight into the pastry.

'Get going with your tarts then come round for a mark when you are done.'

Len and his group snigger. Ah. It's the tart talk that has made them laugh again.

We're quickly done, which is the point of convenience, and they file past carrying plates of tarts piled with pastel coloured foam. It's a joke giving them a mark for following instructions from a packet of chemicals but they've packed them away and they're off.

It's the end of the school day and Cynthia puts the kettle on. We wrap our hands around warm mugs of tea and share a slice of beige, foam-topped tart. A spoonful of creamy, caramelly froth melts in my mouth. Nutritional value of this pudding – bah humbug. Who cares? Thankyou Mr Food Chemist for this taste sensation.

'By the way Cynthia, it's my birthday.'

'Let's click our mugs together and say 'Cheers' Jenny.'

I think if she knew me better she'd give me a hug.

The cheese tasting

'Class, today we're going to make some cheese and have a cheese tasting.'

'Eew, Yuk ... cheese,' comes the grumble from the back of the stools.

I need sour milk for my lesson to show how curdled milk is used to make cheese. I usually squirt lemon juice into fresh milk to make curds, but my food funds are short so I search out old, half empty milk bottles which lurk around the school. They're stashed in places where teachers hide, drink tea, smoke and escape from being caught to cover lessons or do extra break or lunch duties.

Students are round my table and ready to start.

'How do you think people found out how to make cheese?'

'Dunno.'

Gavin hasn't been to my lessons for ages. The relief of having a class without Gavin is enormous. The rest of us can get on and don't have to watch for Gavin's angry outbursts or wanderings around the room, stealing other people's food. This must be his first day back after his recent suspension, but he's not subdued, and he could make this lesson tough going.

I'm into my legends about food. The 'Did you know?' and 'You'll never believe this' type of storytelling that helps them remember the lesson and gets them settled, just like nursery school children.

'According to legend, cheese was invented thousands of years ago when Arab herdsmen carried milk in bags made from sheep's stomachs. By the end of their journey, the milk had turned into cheese. An enzyme called rennet in the sheep's stomach curdled the milk and made curds which then became cheese as the liquid drained away. They'd discovered the art of cheesemaking.'

Please Gavin, don't ask why they put milk in a stomach. Or why the Arabs carry a stomach bag around.

The wooden stool legs squeak. They're getting restless.

'Let's make some cheese. Gavin. Hold this sieve and pour the milk through.'

I can't risk leaving Gavin amongst the stools – I need to watch what he is doing. As Gavin pours, I chant Miss Muffet's nursery rhyme about her eating her curds and whey to distract from the stench of the sour milk. The muslin-lined sieve fills up with creamy lumps.

'Gavin, show the group your curds.'

Gavin tilts the sieve towards the class.

'Can the rest of you see Gavin's curds?'

No-one wants to see anything of Gavin's. He might pin them against a wall later and threaten them.

'Gavin – tie the muslin bag with the curds to the tap and let it drain over the sink, please. At the end of the lesson we'll have a look and taste it.'

'I ain't eating that. It looks like sick.'

It's Liz, the only girl who speaks when Gavin's around. I wonder if something is going on between them. He's huge and she's tiny. If he lay on top of her, she'd die from flattening.

'Write these words in your exercise books to describe for homework.'

My chalk stub makes teeth tingling screeches on the black roller board.

Milk, Sour, Curds, Whey, Rennet, Enzyme, Cheese.

Half the class gets out their pens and exercise books. Half follow Gavin and do nothing. I've printed out homework sheets on the school Banda machine which I'll hand out at the end of the lesson. It's not worth a fight now. Cheese and curds could go everywhere.

'Let's start the cheese tasting.'

For their cheese tasting I've bought large chunks of Cheddar, Caerphilly, Lancashire and Double Gloucester from Budgens supermarket using my tiny food budget. This lesson is educational so they don't pay. Just like they don't pay for chemicals in Chemistry or paint in Art classes. My food budget is running out and I need to talk to the headmaster as more students keep being sent to join my lessons.

Cynthia, my right hand helper, chops the cheeses into tiny pieces and labels them. Equal pieces. Yes, the same size pieces. Pieces that look the same to avoid 'His is bigger... smaller than mine.'

Everyone has a plate, a wooden cocktail stick to spear their cheese chunks, one Jacob's Cream Cracker and a glass of palate-cleansing water. And a tasting chart to fill in with a mark out of ten for each cheese.

I'd like them to learn new tastes but I bet I know the results.

'Which is your favourite cheese, class?'

'Cheddar.'

'What about all the others?'

'We don't like 'em, we only like Cheddar.'

'What cheese would you choose to crumble onto cheese on toast?'

'Cheddar.'

'Why don't you like the other cheeses?'

'Because we like Cheddar.'

I pass round the first plate of tiny pieces of a creamy, mild cheese.

'This Caerphilly cheese is moist and salty. Welsh coal miners need a salty cheese to replace the salt they have lost in sweat when they are working hard in underground mines. When you've finished tasting, eat a piece of cracker and take a sip of water to clean your palate for the next one.'

'Gavin. What now?'

'Got any more biscuits, Miss? To clean my palate?'

Cynthia instinctively snaps the remaining crackers in half. For Gavin and the other boys this cheese tasting is lunch. If they fill up on cheese and crackers, they can go down to the betting shop.

The National Dairy Council is keen to promote cheeses in school and provides booklets and coloured charts to decorate my room. If the class is good, next term we'll go on a trip to their headquarters near Oxford Street for a demonstration. But only if they are good. Really good. And if I can persuade Gavin not to come.

I point to the large wall map called English Cheeses which shows chunks of cheese dotted around England. Caerphilly is shown with an arrow pointing to Wales. Why's that there? And what's happened to cheeses from Scotland or Northern Ireland?

Lancashire cheese is next.

'Lancashire cheese comes from the north of England. It's much colder there and this cheese is used a lot in cooking.'

'Is that where you come from, Miss?'

'No, Len, I come from north of Watford, the Midlands. Not the north.'

They don't get this tease. Watford is an unknown land.

'Crumble this cheese into potato pie and bake in cheese pasties.'

'Don't like it, Miss.'

'Why not?'

Why ask? I know Cheddar will be in the answer.

We move onto orange Double Gloucester, and then golden, solid, reliable Cheddar.

'Now in groups, add up the votes on your charts please.'

They struggle to find a good adding up person. Gavin is munching the spare cream crackers. No one wants his votes.

'What's the favourite cheese from this tasting?'

'Cheddar!' they shout. Of course.

I've got a surprise before they go. From the fridge I take out a wedge of Stilton with its nobbled, crusty rind, and pungent, creamy inside mottled with blue veins.

'Can you see the holes in the rind? The mould grows and spreads through the cheese and gives it a special flavour.'

This is a perfectly delicious piece of Stilton.

'Do any of you want to taste it?'

Even Gavin reels back in horror.

'Why would we eat mouldy, stinky cheese?'

I'm not going to show them the slice of pongy, seeping Brie that I've bought for my lunch. It smells like the boy's toilets and tastes heavenly.

As they pack up ready to leave, I hand them each a National Dairy Council book on cheese making, with the map of English

Cheese including one from Wales, their Banda-ed homework and the recipe for next week, Cheese and potato pie.

But I've forgotten Gavin's curds. The whey is still dripping out through the muslin bag over the sink.

'Does anyone want to taste these curds?'

'Na, thanks. Told you it's like sick.' Liz links arms with Gavin and leaves.

'Alright, well you might want to pop in later and see how I've made the curd into Yorkshire curd tarts.'

Tarts, tarts. I know Len likes tarts, so he might be back, even though he's left his homework sheet on the window ledge.

It's time for my visit to the staffroom like I promised Mr Lewes. I slump into one of the armchairs, light up a cigarette and breathe out 'Gavin.' in a stream of smoke.

'Ah, Jenny. Gavin is being suspended again because he's been threatening boys in the cloakroom.'

It's friendly teacher Pete who often pops in to see if I can sell him anything for his supper.

'When the school disciplinary team interviewed him, he told them he likes your lessons the best. They'll suspend him for a week and he can come back and join another of your classes. Mr James is supposed to tell you.'

Brilliant. Gavin is the school tormenter and general nuisance maker. He spends much of his time outside classroom doors, roaming the corridors or waiting near the headmaster's study for a telling off or more serious stuff. Rumour has it that Mr Shield once chased him around the room waving his cane, but Gavin escaped. That made us all laugh. The Team, whoever they are, has decided he can spend time with me as he likes cooking. Gavin refuses to bring in ingredients and ends up making jam tarts or stealing stuff from other students. And I've got to get the rest of the class through EXAMS.

Tonight Mark has bought two tickets to the musical 'Godspell' and we'll drive into the West End and have bowls of noodles and spicy pork in Chinatown before the show. Reviews say it's a jolly musical with energetic young people dancing and singing, dressed in clown costumes. The pop star, David Essex is playing Jesus – he's got the most startling blue eyes and is screamingly handsome. I know the ending's sad as Jesus dies, but I'm not going to let that spoil my night out. We've been playing the Godspell LP so might join in a quiet singalong as we know the words. Prepare Ye The Way of the Lord, Day by Day – here we come.

Rough poof pastry

Rough puff pastry is a highly regarded skill revered by visiting cookery examiners and I must teach it. This high fat, high calorie, greasy recipe has many health issues, enhanced by making sausage rolls with cheap, fatty pork sausage meat and twirling pastry into cream horns filled with jam and whipped cream.

Jim, the caretaker, is testing the heating system, blasting hot water through the ancient radiators and my room is hot. Very hot.

Hot is not good for pastry making.

My students gather round my demonstration table watching me drop lumps of lard and margarine into a bowl of flour.

'Cut the fat into walnut sized lumps then drop them into the flour.'

'What size is a walnut Miss?'

Alice is always challenging. But she's right, and she's keen – if you don't know the size of a walnut you don't know the size of my lumps.

'This big.' I hold up a piece of squashed fat and drop it into the bowl.

'Add cold water, then work it together with your hands to make a soft dough.'

It's sticky and squelchy and they are pleased to watch me struggle.

'Why is it called rough poof pastry Miss?'

Bert, the class comic, swirls round to the group, smirking for approval. I give him my shut up look, but he carries on.

'Miss, we're always making really rude things in your lessons. Spotted dick, fruity tarts and now this poof pastry.'

Len is nudging Bert and enjoying the tease. It is hot. Very hot.

Cooking is full of rudeness. You rub things in, knock pastry up, wait while dough rises, but I have to teach them the correct terms.

'Should I leave this to rise, Miss?'

'Can you check if this is knocked up?'

This comic banter from the boys progresses into guffaws and reaches a peak when someone falls off their stool, bringing the lesson to a halt.

'Bert, if you keep this up, you'll leave the room.'

'Keep what up, Miss?' The faces of Bert and his chums redden with laughter.

The girls in this group are quieter and kinder. I must say thankyou to them.

'Class, these are proper cooking terms and you have to know what they mean. Knocking up and rubbing in are things you need to learn.'

'Oh yes' mutters Len. 'We'll learn.'

They must not get the better of me, especially when it is so hot.

Very hot.

After weeks at this school I am still unfamiliar with east London josh. My worst moment comes during the school versus teachers hockey match when I wear my University sweatshirt.

BRISTOL UNIVERSITY stretches in large letters across my chest. Students at the touchline giggle as I approach the boundary lines.

'What are they laughing at?' I ask Pete after the game.

'They think you have been to university to study Bristols.' he replies.

'Bristols are tits. Cockney rhyming slang – Bristol City – titty.'

The offending sweatshirt gets packed away after the match which we lost.

Back in my sweltering cookery room they squidge and squash the fat into flour and add water to make a pastry mash. This is a hot sweaty room with hot sweaty hands, and the dough looks like we feel. Hot and sweaty.

I don't care if the Stork Cookery Service has tested this recipe. This is a pointless, purposeless cooking activity. Those Stork people have never tried it with a class of teenagers in a hot, airless cookery room with Jim banging on the radiators.

I've had enough. They have had enough.

'Wrap and label your pastry, wash up and take your Stork Cookery books outside and read about Rough Puff Pastry.'

I hand out Duralex glasses filled with orange squash and pass round a plate of McVitie's digestive biscuits on a frilly d'oyley. Always a bloody d'oyley. Standards must be maintained, even when it's hot. They sit in the sunshine on the steps outside my room. Before I go home I pack their pieces of pastry into the freezer for next time. Rough poof pastry can wait till another day. Bugger it.

A week later the room is still hot. Very hot. But the pastry is cold, ice cold.

'You haven't defrosted it properly, Miss. Did you forget to take them out of the freezer 'cos you were so busy with your boyfriend last night?'

Carol is being smart and nosy again. But she's right. Mark and I joined friends at a gig to hear a lively folk group called Steeleye Span and I arrived at school a bit late and muddled today.

We roll and fold the cold dough then roll and fold some more, creating magic layers. The ovens must be hot, very hot, ready for this baking bonanza.

We make the pastry into so many things – sausage rolls, cheese straws, Eccles cakes and jam puffs, to display our high levels of skill for the EXAM. Spare pastry is cut into strips and twisted round cream horn tins. These rusting metal pyramids have been lurking in the school storeroom since the school opened in the fifties. No amount of scouring with Brillo pads removes the brown dust which lingers in the cracks and I just hope the heat of the oven kills off germs.

Next year I'll throw them away, along with the iron griddles for drop scones, fish kettles for unaffordable salmon, raised pork pie moulds and chocolate éclair tins. I'm sure one day they will appear in an antique shop window at an astonishing price which reflects their culinary history.

Sausage rolls are glazed and snipped, sugary milk is brushed onto Eccles cakes, jam puffs and cream horns and baking trays are stacked with pastries then into the scorching ovens.

Suddenly we're ready. The Eccles cakes have a crusty, sugary topping, ooze currants and mixed peel and the spicy fragrance of cinnamon. They outshine the golden gloss of the sausage rolls.

'Put them on cooling racks for marking and collect after school.'

The bell rings.

They grab their coats and rush.

Onto the next lesson.

Mustn't be late.

'Mr Smith in Maths gets cross, Miss.'

No amount of feeding Mr Smith tidbits can persuade him that my class should stay and clear up.

But we have learnt about rough poof pastry and it's one more skill ticked off for the EXAM.

Wearily Cynthia and I patrol the cookers and lift out the remaining pastries. Dirty baking trays are piled into sinks filled with soapy suds in the hope that their owners will return. If not,

Cynthia and I must scrub our way through lunchtime and get ready for the eager cooks who are making Scandinavian Tea Ring from *Cooking is Fun*. I notice someone has crossed out Fun and scrawled in Horrible. I hope I can change their mind.

Autumn Half Term 1972

Rosehips

It's half term week and I drive up the M1 from London to Kettering to visit my family, especially my grandmother. Autumn, season of mists and mellow fruitfulness, is my favourite time of year and as October is my birthday month, it's a month that matters.

Every time I go home I drive my mother to Leicester market. The fabric stalls are such a treat. Leicester is a great textile manufacturing city and the tables are piled with rolls of the latest designs used in the fashion shops in London. I buy yards of flowered crimplene for a frock, silky polyester for a blouse, and some strange black and white stuff for a garment of my invention. Sewing and the radio are my companions in the empty days of my home visits and I rattle away on my mother's electric Singer sewing machine making new stuff for my wardrobe. Eat your heart out Barbara Hulanicki and Vivienne Westwood. I'm making Biba copies and Westwood ragged skirts. This Kettering fashionista is returning to London with shorter hemlines, a pair of thigh high brown suede boots and the shortest purple suede skirt on Leicester market. I discover later that the purple dye comes off on my legs and makes them look bruised and stains the fabric on my mother's favourite settee when I sit down.

Before I go back, we drive around the country lanes doing some wild foraging. I'm going to show the students hawthorn berries and bitter sloes, and we pick branches of rosehips and some wild crab apples.

My first paid job as a child was collecting rosehips to take to

Park Road Infants School to sell for thrupence a pound. Every weekend in October, I made my parents and grandmother drive out to the countryside and we'd pick the hips from the prickly bushes. The thorns spiked our skins and tore at our clothes, but I wanted to win the school prize for picking the most. Each week I lost out to Malcolm who lived in a farmhouse near a huge row of rosehip bushes, and he spent his evenings out picking me. Weekday evenings were too dark for my parents to drive out to the countryside, however hard I begged, and anyway they both had jobs and were tired after work.

In those days kids were given a teaspoon of rosehip syrup for our daily boost of vitamin C as supplies of oranges and lemons were scarce after the war. Each morning my mother would top me up with a teaspoon of National Health Orange and a horrid, greasy spoonful of cod liver oil. 'For vitamin A Jenny.' Ugh, it was awful. The nation needed to find local sources of vitamin C to keep us healthy and said that rosehips contained twenty times the vitamin C of an orange. It's strange how small children became the cheap labour force and created the school rosehip mountain which was sent to the Delrosa factory, then turned into a very sweet Delrosa Rosehip Syrup.

My rosehips should make an interesting start to my lesson on Vitamins. As long as the boys don't steal them and use the seeds for itching powder.

The breakup

The journey back down the M1 at the end of half term is eventful. My unreliable Mini Traveller, filled with windfall apples and pears from my grandmother's garden, limps onto the hard shoulder and expires. Surely my AA silver badge fitted to the bumper will come to the rescue even though I haven't paid the membership? The yellow AA van draws up and the kindly AA man pops his head under the bonnet.

'Haven't I seen you before on this road?' It's true. My car struggles to make it past the Watford Gap Service Station without a whimper.

'Shall I top you up with petrol?' Kind man. He's had a poke around in the bonnet but running out of petrol is the most likely breakdown reason.

'Next time let the AA know when you're travelling and we'll look out for you.'

Not sure how, but that's generous. We've no phone in the Kettering bungalow and I haven't passed a phone box on the M1. Perhaps I should join or make a large yellow flag.

Onto Hampstead and to surprise Mark as I'm back a day early from my holiday. Our flat is at the top of four flights of stairs and I'm puffed when I open our front door. Mark is in the hall and seems very flustered when I rush to hug him. Beside him stands a large suitcase with pulley wheels and a lift up plastic handle. Smart. New.

'?? Whose is this?' Silence.

'Is someone staying here? IN OUR FLAT?'

A tall, elegant woman emerges from the bathroom. Long, dark hair hangs down her back and she's rather beautiful.

'Sandy!'

I remember Sandy from our summer backpacking holiday in Corfu. Sandy from Ohio. She had that bloody wheely suitcase there. While the rest of us humped our belongings around in rucksacks, bloody American Sandy got help unloading her suitcase down the bus steps. Steve from our group pulled it up the dusty road to the taverna where we were all staying. And then Sandy joined us for jolly suppers and shared our ouzo.

'Yes, Jenny. Just popped by on my way to France – wanted to say hello to you both. Going back to the States now.'

Mark scoops up the suitcase and lumbers down the stairs. Sandy follows quickly behind.

At the outside door he shouts back.

'Just taking Sandy to the station – back soon.'

Agghh! Sandy.

The covers on top of our brass bed are rumpled. Sandy has been staying and Mark is due for a Goldilocks style interrogation. WHO'S BEEN SLEEPING IN MY BED?

From now on Mark must sleep on the sofa. I don't care that it's too short so he must hang his legs over the arms. He's not coming near our double bed while I'm in it. But first I take all of the bed linen down to the launderette to wash and get rid of Sandy's smell.

I'm hurt at his infidelity. We seemed to have high hopes for a future together, but I can't trust a man who hooks up with Sandy and I've got to leave.

The bedsit

The *Evening Standard* has regular adverts for house sharing and vacant bedsits. I won't go too far. Mark and I can keep in touch and still be friends after all this time together. And maybe we can make up. It's a big maybe.

At the weekend he helps me move my stuff into my new bedsit. It's hardly new – just a large room decorated with red flock wallpaper on the first floor overlooking the street trees. These Hampstead houses were very grand before they divided them into single bedsit rooms, each door with its own yale and chubb lock. The landlord says that there's no phone in the house. Previous tenants used it unreasonably so he's cut off the line but I'll find a phone box down in the main road. Letters are left on the entrance hall table and we're all responsible for keeping the house clean. And no visitors after 9 o'clock or staying overnight. So will the other bedsit inhabitants, hiding behind their locked doors, snitch and tell tales to the landlord?

'That new woman had someone in her room and they used our toilet.'

Fat chance I'd want to bring anyone back to this dismal place. My room has a one ring Baby Belling with a tiny oven just big enough to heat up a small meat pie. The house has no fridge and I'll share the bathroom and separate toilet with Michael and Sam who live in the other rooms on my floor. Since the toilet has no washbasin – 0/10 for hygiene – I'll have to use the pink hand basin in my room, which doubles as my washing up sink for my single plate, cup and bowl. Sad. The landlord is proud that electricity bills are included in the rent and he's left me a one bar electric fire which doesn't look like it will raise the room temperature much on winter nights. Although it might set fire to my nightie if I get too close. At least my milk won't go sour if this chill in my room continues.

Mark seems rather deflated as he heads back to our comfortable flat, but I'm not staying with a man who invites someone round the moment I head up the M1. He'll have some serious apologising to do before I consider spending much time with him again. And I'm not sure how I will trust him.

The single bed in the corner of my bedsit is a sad reflection of my new life. This is not a home or a place to bring back visitors. And certainly not a place for noisy dinner parties.

Meantime I can plan my lessons, mark their homework and cope with a very demanding job in a challenging school. Oh, the fun of being single in swinging London. I'm going to continue taking my daily contraceptive pill, just in case things perk up.

My grandmother's cooking

My grandmother is the person that showed me how to cook, and her recipes are trapped in a time warp of the *Be-Ro Home Recipes* with its battered, grease stained pages.

Born in 1883, she lives frugally on her small state pension in the terraced house in Kettering which her husband bought in 1920 after coming back from the war. Before her marriage, she worked as a laundry maid in a large house in Wimbledon, and once went on a day trip to France with the family, where she learnt her one French word, *fromage*. She only travelled abroad once and is proud that she still remembers a foreign word.

My grandmother's large garden is the joy of her life, and I spend many childhood hours with her when my mother cycles off to her teaching job in the secondary modern school. Together we gather, prepare and cook her fruit and vegetables. Grandma has no refrigerator, and stores perishable things like milk and butter in the cool of a lead-lined cabinet on the marble shelf in her larder. Spare fruit is made into jams, chutneys and pickles and in autumn we peel her hard, green Conference pears, stack the long slices in large glass Kilner jars then top up with hot sugar syrup spiced with dark brown cloves. They stand proudly in her larder next to jars of pink Victoria plums, waiting to be made into puddings when the garden is winter quiet. Her cooking apples make chutney which joins pots of glowing-red crab apple jelly and strawberry and raspberry jam. A feast ready to tide us through winter until the garden comes to life in spring.

In early autumn, Grandma's trees hang with pink, wasp infested Victoria plums, and her ancient variety of mottled apple which she cooks to a creamy pulp for her buttery apple charlotte.

September 1966 is a date for Grandma to remember. I bring my friend Peter to help me gather her fruit. He climbs up the ladder propped against her giant Conference pear tree as she gazes up after him.

'I've never had a black man pick my pears before' she whispers as we fill baskets with fruit to bottle later. Grandma has never seen a black man in Kettering and she really likes Peter.

In spring we pick the first leafy mint shoots, chop them finely with sugar, and mix with pungent Sarson's vinegar. Grandma only uses cooking ingredients with the best trade names. Be-Ro flour, Saxa salt, Lion brand white pepper, Colman's mustard, Tate and

Lyle sugar, Bisto gravy powder, Borwick's baking powder and Bird's custard. Spring brings her delicate pink rhubarb which is forced under metal buckets so that it grows sweet and tender. We pick, chop and stew it with sugar and eat it with bowls of thick, yellow Bird's custard.

Spears of asparagus poke through the ground in early May and Grandma cuts the stems from deep in the soil with her sharp knife and pops them in a pan of boiling water. By mid-summer her garden fills with ripening gooseberries and blackcurrants. We sit in the sunshine on her wooden kitchen chairs gently 'topping and tailing' the spiky ends into an aluminium bowl. The fruit is stewed for pies and crumbles or made into jam ready for winter toast and butter around her fire.

In high summer there are strawberries, grown through layers of dry, yellow straw, and covered with black cotton net.

'Tread carefully and don't squash them, Jenny. Pick only the red ones and put that net back and peg it down. We don't want that blackbird pecking our fruit.'

Birds and cats get shouted, stoned and clapped out of her garden. She keeps a pile of stones by her back door just for this purpose.

Strawberries only grow for a few weeks and we hull, slice, and sprinkle them with fine sugar mixed with thick Jersey cream, to eat from special glass bowls.

Raspberries grow in a cage covered in a fine green net, which still traps the birds inside, making Grandma jump around clapping her hands in fury. Grandma's raspberries are full of tiny white maggots which I squish under my seat.

'They won't harm you, Jenny – they've only been eating raspberries.'

'I had three London children here to stay during the war as evacuees. We had to manage on food rations then so my garden was really useful. I know London children can be cheeky but you'll get the better of them soon and they love to cook. They drove up once to visit me and bring their own children. I hadn't realised how many years had passed.'

It seems funny that we Londoners are still sharing the fruits from her garden.

The Loose Box

'You need to get out more – go to places where attractive men hang out.'

This is my younger, lovely sister with her pin-up qualities and billowing blond hair, who never needs to pick up any man. They just swarm. We meet at The Loose Box, the new wine bar in Knightsbridge. Wine bars are the latest hangouts for young people who don't want to visit dingy London pubs, like the one near my school. In The Loose Box we perch on stools at high tables, and sip Cotes du Rhone by candlelight and wait for potential talent to walk in.

'Tonight we'll speak to men who have jobs beginning with A-C. So that's Architects, Accountants, Bank Managers, Chartered Surveyors,' she orders.

It's a good plan but I'll probably end up with a Butcher or Chip shop owner and she'll get the posh Artist or City Trader. By the Christmas holidays my target is to get to C in my job alphabet search and hopefully find someone to date.

'So that's no Teachers, Undertakers or Window cleaners till July, Jenny.' I hope it doesn't take that long.

'Would you like a top up ladies?'

Two expensively suited, well groomed young men approach. One of them is wearing a wide kipper tie that matches the handkerchief pointing out of his top jacket pocket. Seems a bit dapper.

They hold up a bottle of Chablis. The frosty glass looks beautifully chilled and a drink seems like a good offer.

'Hello – what do you two do?' Perhaps that's a bit bold of me but we're off and it's started. My glass of wine is cool and tastes expensive. This dating business is going to be bloody hard work.

At these times of stress a cigarette will calm me down but no-one is smoking in the bar and if I bring out my packet of Embassy it might look a bit common. Mark smokes smart Benson and Hedges cigarettes with their beautiful golden box and when we lived together I'd pick a pack from his pile and never bought my own. Now I'm alone, I've swapped to the cheaper brand of Embassy, and on poorer days it's Player's No 6 which comes in a box of ten. If I'm hanging about in posh wine bars it's time to smarten up my smoking. There are two choices for my cigarette experiment. The beautiful blue and white packet of Rothmans King Size with its long cigarettes inside and those green packs of Consulate menthol with that advert girl saying 'Cool as a mountain stream'. I'll get advice from my staffroom smoking chums.

The wine was nice but the two men are dull so we're off. It's a tricky drive from Knightsbridge back to north London and I mustn't drink too much before my early morning start at school.

Egg magic

Eggs are teaching magic. My science degree will impress them – a little biology, some physics and a bit of bird watching along the way. The egg is the centre of my cooking world, the source of endless cheap dishes, and a great way to teach nutrition.

'Go to work on an egg' is the advert from The Egg Marketing Board found in newspapers and magazines. If I have an egg, I have a lesson, and even a breakfast to go to work on – or in my case, to boil up when I get to school.

'Gather round and stand in a circle – I'm going to show you a trick.'

I roll the egg gently in the centre of the floor. It curls, curves and circles back to me.

'Look at that for magic – in nature it rolls back if it falls out of the nest.'

I've got their attention. Later I'll shock them with tales of poor, beak-clipped battery chickens stuck in cages that never see a nest or daylight and lay most of the eggs that we buy. I've visited an egg farm and seen how their eggs drop through the bars of their prison cages and down into collecting tubes. These sad, featherless birds blinked at me for rescue. Their next stop was the chicken pie factory and they don't need plucking. Battery farming makes eggs cheap and perfect for low budget recipes and the public doesn't care.

Eggs used to have the Little Lion symbol stamped on their shells but my box of eggs gives no clues about when or where the eggs have been laid. But I have a DATE TEST.

'How do you know if an egg is fresh Alice?'

I've been neglecting the girls in my classes and must give them more attention. The boisterous boys shoot up their hands or shout out when I ask a question.

'Boys, wait for Alice to answer, please.'

Quiet, gentle Alice stands up to answer. She's surrounded by boy cries of 'Ask me, ask me.' 'I know.'

I ignore the boys' enthusiasm. My girls matter in this thrusting, testosterone-filled world, and I must give them a chance.

Ray can't contain himself any more.

'Miss, you can smell if it's off – it stinks. Old eggs are good for stink bombs.'

I give Ray a stern look. He's right. An off egg has the disgusting smell of sulphur.

It's the girls' turn. They must not be bullied into silence.

'Alice, come and help me with the egg test.'

She stands nervously by the large jug of salty water on my demonstration table. I hand her three eggs. Two are new purchases and the other from the old egg collection hidden in the storeroom. Sometimes, I forget they are there, and they mature into stink bombs.

'Alice, drop each egg carefully into a jug of salted water – the fresh eggs sink and the stale egg floats.'

One of the eggs bobs to the top and the others are suspended midway.

'See, this floating egg is stale so we don't use it. Thankyou Alice for helping.'

Miss the Magician has done it again. And I've let the girls have a turn. This lesson is going well and I've got more egg tricks to share which will take this session into the stratosphere.

'Did you know that whole eggs are passed over a light to see if they are clear inside with no bloody bits or chicks growing? It's called candling and you can do it with a candle. Alice, can you hold the candle and light it, please?'

I hold my egg in front of her candle flame. The egg shell shines and the candle flame is hot. You can't see through it like The British Egg Information photo. This piece of magic proves that the egg shell shines golden, and that candle flame is hot. I'm no better at tricks than Tommy Cooper.

OK. Go back to your places.'

Cynthia has given them each an egg, a green Beryl Ware saucer and a dinner knife.

'Aren't we cooking today, Miss? I don't want theory.'

Len struggles with reading and writing and he tells me he can 'do' cookery but not other lessons. I wonder how he will manage in the adult world with no Maths or English qualifications.

'Len, we'll cook when we've finished this bit.'

'And Miss, I want a brown egg, not a white one. Brown eggs are better.'

I can feel the class nodding and preparing to swap their white eggs for brown.

'Look – you don't eat the shell, so it doesn't matter. Now crack your egg in half and slide the contents onto the saucer. I'm going to give you a biology lesson. See the air sac in the top of the shell.'

The egg shell is lined with a thin white membrane with a bubble at the top.

'This is where the chick takes its first breath before it pecks its way out.'

'Do we ever get chicks in our eggs then?' Len's enthusiasm is returning.

'It's OK – there are no chicks in these eggs. They've been reared in cages with no cockerels around.'

Hens, cockerels and chicks? Which reminds me. I'm teaching a sex education lesson next week and need some condoms and cucumbers. And I expect a few boyfriend questions.

They crack their eggs onto saucers and poke the air sac in the shell.

'Look at the yolk. Can you see the germ – the tiny white circle where the chick grows?'

'You said this egg won't be a chick?'

Len wants to get on with COOKING.

'See the two chords – the chalaza – which hold the yolk in place. And the thick and thin whites.'

They peer at their saucers. What's the point in this?

'Miss, when are we cooking?'

Ray has reared his head this time.

'Label a cross section of an egg' is a popular EXAM question, so I'm showing you what it really looks like.'

Here she goes again. The EXAM – everything is learnt to pass the bloody EXAM.

'We're ready to make chocolate mousse – it's just raw egg and chocolate.'

'Put the yolk into a bowl then whisk the egg white in another bowl until it is stiff. When it's ready turn the bowl upside down and the egg whites stay in.'

This is the most stupid test of all. If they turn the bowl over too early the whole lot plops out and the sticky mess streams over the floor accompanied by screams of hilarity. We must start again. Thank goodness eggs are cheap.

Chocolate mousse is easy. Good mousses are light and fluffy. Bad mousses are a runny mess.

'Melt the chocolate in a bowl over a saucepan of hot water, stir in the yolk and then fold the melted chocolate gently into the whisked whites – gently.'

They pile the soft, brown mixture into glass dishes on a saucer with a frilly d'oyley, top with a glacé cherry and bring round for marking. Someone should make Beryl Ware with a d'oyley imprint, just for school exams. The mousse must not leave the classroom. It has to be eaten or scraped in the bin. I don't want the bus company complaining of sticky seats after my cooking class has travelled home.

At the end of school, Dawn pops her head round the door.

'Good news Jenny. Mr Shield has reviewed your capitation and is increasing your food funds.'

She hands me a note with some numbers written down and raises a grin.

'He says you can afford to provide ingredients for those who don't bring them to school.' I think she meant to say 'those boys.'

'Try and collect money for their cooking and bring the coins for me to bank each week.'

Great. Success. But I want more. More time for Cynthia. More up to date textbooks. More modern kitchen equipment. If the Science department can have those beautiful wooden boxes full of microscopes and Maths has class sets of calculators, then I want some electric whisks.

It's late on a Friday afternoon when I've cleared up and a gaggle of staff pass by my room.

'Come on Jenny. Join us at the pub for a drink and meet up in the Saloon.'

Why does this offer to walk down to the parade of shops, into the drab building, across its sticky carpet to an even stickier wooden table in the Saloon seem so unappealing?

I visited this pub once before at lunchtime and made my way

through the smoky gloom to the Public Bar. A group of old men perched on stools blocked the small space for serving customers and when I leant on the bar to order a shandy my hands stuck to the rings of dried beer spills. Clearly a place of general stickiness.

But tonight I'm going. Mr Lewes is going too and he said it will be good for me to join in. It will surely be better than a night in my bedsit.

The evening passes with laughter and gossip, pints of beer and packets of crisps. Two of the younger men teachers who live alone have agreed to buy any of my demonstration dishes for their supper. And I decide that if ever my dating by job search gets to T, it will not include teachers.

On the shelf

I've had a small party with friends in their flat to celebrate my birthday. I'm twenty four. Twenty four. On the shelf. Unmarried, single and I don't even know which shelf I've been put on. Even the equipment and ingredients in my school storeroom have a special shelf. My Kettering friends warn me that all the best men get picked off if I don't hurry up, so it's time to find my shelf and let them sniff about, dust me off and take me down for inspection.

Mr Jones, the head of Maths, has been doing some sniffing in the breaktime coffee queue.

'You know Jenny, you're the best looking of the new women teachers who started this term.'

There are two reasons why Mr Jones can't look on my shelf. First, he's married and second, I saw him get into a noisy confrontation with a group of boys and bat one of them round the head.

Tonight we're meeting at my girlfriends' flat to work on our Getting off the Shelf plans.

It's decided. A shopping day – a bus down to Oxford Street, starting with a cookery demonstration at Selfridges, a bus to

Knightsbridge to zip up Harrods escalators to the fourth floor and Way In, their noisy boutique with edgy displays of fashions for men and women. Down to the ground floor into the fabulous Food Hall with samples of cheese, salami and other nibbles to curb our hunger. Another bus and we're in the King's Road sitting at pavement tables eating ice creams with fan shaped wafers served in cut glass sundae dishes and watching the world of fashion parade past. We gaze like children outside a sweet shop into Mary Quant's Bazaar shop window. It feels too expensive and intimidating to go through the door so we head off to the bustling fun of Chelsea Girl boutique. Then back on the bus and home. It didn't quite meet the Getting off the Shelf plan but we had loads of fun and we're having fish and chips with loads of vinegar and salt and eating them out of the newspaper for supper.

Beaujolais Nouveau

November 15th is Beaujolais Nouveau Day and it's a great race from France to London to see who can arrive and open the first bottle. Mark has invited me to celebrate the event at his friend Peter's wine bar. Thank god it's not at The Loose Box where I might bump into one of my A-C list of male pickups.

The *Evening Standard* headline blasts -

'Le Beaujolais Nouveau est arrivé.'

A small crowd gathers outside as an ancient Jaguar races towards us. Peter leaps out waving hands full of bottles which he proudly clanks together. We cheer and raise our empty glasses in readiness. It has arrivéd.

'We've been on the ferry from Calais and I've sped through Kent to get here. Am I one of the first?'

We don't care if he's first or last. The crowd just wants to taste this fruity, young wine, which is ready to drink just weeks after the grape harvest. It may be a PR stunt but we Londoners love this fun. Then it's on to The Hot Pot in Earl's Court to share a casserole of Coq au Vin and bottles of French Vin de Table. Good food always cheers me up and Mark seems hopeful of us getting back together. There are a few letters left in my Loose Box date-search to complete first.

I never taught chicken

In the 1970s we never cook chicken in school lessons. It is just too expensive and only eaten for special days like Christmas and Easter.

Our main textbook does not even have chicken in the index and the other one says that chicken is 'chiefly eaten for easily digested animal protein, especially for an invalid diet.'

One afternoon, Alan drifts into my room with a plastic carrier bag containing a trussed chicken, some muddy potatoes and a block of dripping, all wrapped in damp newspaper.

Alan doesn't do school.

He doesn't do his hair or take his grubby anorak off.

And sometimes he doesn't do his flies up.

Alan never does my homework or any other homework for that matter.

'Alan, we can't afford to cook chicken. It's too dear. Where did you get it from?'

I want to say '... nicked it from' but that is a bit near the knuckle.

I've never ever cooked a chicken in my life so I can't help him.

'Find a recipe in my books for roast chicken and you can follow that.'

The rest of the class is busy making shepherd's pie, and Alan's roast chicken is a nuisance. A bit showy off, but this is a surprise visit to my lesson and he needs encouragement to cook.

Marguerite Patten's *Cookery in Colour* takes him through the recipe in simple steps.

As the rest of us mash potatoes, the room fills with the rare, delicious smells of roasting chicken.

Skin crispening to golden, chicken breast softening to melt point, and legs ready to rip off and ooze juice.

The chicken nests in a circle of crunchy, roast potatoes which Alan occasionally bastes with melted dripping. Crisp, golden potatoes, with crisp golden chicken. Yum.

I comfort the rest of the class.

'We don't need to learn about chicken. You'll never be asked any questions about it in the exam, and it's in none of our textbooks. And there are no recipes for chicken in *Cooking is Fun*. It's too expensive.'

I scowl as Alan brings over the roasting tin and holds out his sizzling feast.

'Can you mark this Miss, and I'll eat it now?'

No sharing, no offer of the smallest taste. Alan doesn't even lay the table. He carves off hot chicken chucks onto a plate, surrounds it with roasties then gobbles it down, wraps the remains in my tin foil, packs up and leaves.

'TaTa Miss, thanks.'

That night Mark takes me to Villa Bianca in Hampstead. Can I forgive a man who let Sandy stay in our double bed when I was away? Sandy, that American with her suitcase on wheels that so many men pulled for her on our Greek island. Sandy, who stayed in my bed with Mark in it. He's paying tonight as I reckon he owes me. It's not much fun living in a bedsit.

It's all very Italian here – the waiters, the menu, the Chianti wine in its beautiful straw basket. Mark says we're paying for the straw and not what's inside the bottle contents. Wonder if he told that to Sandy.

The smell of Alan's roasting chicken is still narking so I'm ordering their popular chicken dish – Pollo Sorpresa. Crusty, golden, breadcrumbed chicken breast stuffed with garlic butter. The waiter takes a sharp knife, pierces the crust and cuts the first slice. Fragrant, garlicy butter oozes onto the fried potatoes. Thank goodness it didn't splatter over my new blouse. I reckon this could be a popular recipe in the future, especially with the new plug-in deep fat fryers in the shops. There's one last piece of theatre as the waiter brings over a tray with two glasses of flaming Sambuca. This warm, aniseedy drink is a fitting end to a friendly evening.

Mark leaves me at my bedsit house. 'I'd really like another evening with you soon, Jenny. And another.'

He ain't getting away with the Sandy thing yet. I need someone who is trustworthy.

Awful offal

I have to teach offal – it's on the syllabus, and I face these lessons with dread. How can I persuade a class of teenage boys and girls that liver, kidney and hearts are nutritious foods that they must learn to cook for their exams?

As a child our Wednesday night meal was leathery liver and bacon. The later my father and I arrived home, the longer the liver simmered to a texture of old cardboard. The bits that stuck outside the globby gravy were curled and crisp. Only the creamy mashed potato rescued the meal from being scooped into my handkerchief, to throw into the garden later.

Liver, hearts and kidneys are cheap, nutritious foods and excellent sources of iron so I must teach my class how to cook them. The butcher delivers twenty lamb's hearts for today's stuffed hearts lesson and I've bought some Paxo parsley and thyme stuffing, onions, Oxo cubes and flour to finish the recipe. 'Oxo gives a meal man appeal' according to the adverts and any encouragement to cook this dish is essential.

They perch on stools round my demonstration table but there are groans of 'I ain't eating that' as they push for a place on the stools at the back.

A small, pink lamb's heart sits forlornly on the wooden chopping board.

Len speaks for the group.

'Are we cooking that today, Miss? Looks like something I feed me ferrets.'

'I'd give it to me dogs.' chirps Ray.

Cackles of laughter from the rest of the stools.

'Today, we are going to learn to cook with offal.'

I hold up a copy of our textbook bible, *O Level Cookery,* with its red cover, the colour of blood. And I read.

'Offal used to be despised and was very cheap, but because of its increased use and realisation of its high food value it is now popular and more expensive. Offal includes kidneys, tripe, liver, heart, sweetbreads, brain and tongue.'

'See, more people are using it, so we must too. We're making stuffed hearts – a delicious, cheap, family supper dish, and we're going to learn a bit of biology on the way.'

I start to peel off the stiff, fatty bits around the heart and cut the tubes that pop out the top. I give the heart a squeeze, and a clot of blood oozes out the large blood vessel that protrudes from the top.

'Look at this strong heart muscle that pushes blood through the arteries and around the lamb.'

'Oh my god. I feel sick'

It's Carol, who as usual, is disgusted.

'Miss, one week we learn about vegetarians not eating meat, and next we're chopping up lamb's bits and saying they're good for us.'

She gets a scowl as I fill the two pouches with Paxo stuffing. This heart looks like it's just come from a really tiny lamb. Baaa.

'Fry some onions then we'll roast it in a little Oxo gravy. It'll taste really nice.'

It's time to cook but they're stuck to their stools.

'Please get started – the sooner we begin the quicker it's done.

Let's share the tasks – girls can cook the onions and boys can stuff the hearts.'

The girls shuffle off sadly to chop and fry the onions.

Len, Ray and their crowd begin the heart dissection. They are quite enjoying this.

They stuff Paxo into the cavities then the hearts join the fried onions in roasting tins with gravy.

The room warms with the nourishing smells of tiny pieces of roasting meat – or is it roast offal?

The end of lesson bell goes and they are off.

'We'll come back after school and fetch it, Miss.' Len calls as they leave.

I sweep up the bits of fat, heart tubes and onion skins.

At the end of school, I line up the dishes for collection.

And wait.

Len pops his head round the door.

'Sorry Miss – we won't eat it. Why don't you sell it to one of the teachers?'

I put some tiny hearts into foil dishes and trundle into the smoke filled staffroom.

'Would anyone like to buy some stuffed hearts for supper?'

Pete and Adam wander over and lift the foil lid.

'Yum, smells lovely, yes please.'

This is the last stuffed hearts lesson I'll ever teach.

We'll have to use liver for the awful offal lesson instead.

Later I learn that lamb's hearts are an important ingredient in dog food, so my students are right – if you don't like them, they end up as the dog's dinner.

The day my hair caught fire

Our school gas ovens have a small pilot light inside at the back of the oven which stays alight. When you turn on the oven switch, the gas burner inside the oven booms into action.

Today is a busy shortcrust pastry lesson with all three shelves in all twelve ovens operating at full blast and soon the ovens will be stacked with cheese straws, sausage rolls, apple turnovers and multicoloured jam tarts. We need to work quickly to get everything cooked before the end of the lesson.

Ray calls me over.

'Miss, me oven won't light.'

We're late. They've dithered with rolling out pastry and filling their baking trays and there are lots to cook before the bell goes. I speed over, light the taper from the pilot light on the hob and open the oven door. Bang. Boom. The oven explodes and a wall of flame rushes over me. There's a strong, burning smell. As I touch my head, clumps of singed hair fall to the floor and bits of nylon overall melt into brown, crisp pieces.

I stumble shocked, back to my desk as the class cooks on. The bell will go soon, and the room is a tip. I have to carry on.

'Are you alright Miss?' Ray stares at my face and seems alarmed.

Is he worried for his cooking or me?

'Yes, yes – just put your cooking in another oven.'

I reel around bashing down bits of smouldering hair and ripping off my burnt overall.

Around the room the array of amazing pastries piles on wire cooling racks. Sinks are full of washing up, more pastries to cook and I'm feeling weird.

'Sorry class, clear up, give yourself a mark, and pack up and go.'

The bell goes and they rush out, some of them stuffing cheese straws and jam tarts into their mouths, unaware that their teacher has been blown up and burned.

The mirror in the school flat reflects the damage – my face is stripped of eyebrows and eyelashes and the front part of my hair is missing. I'm lucky my contact lenses didn't fuse to my eyeballs.

Ray has stayed behind, waiting for his tarts to cook. He looks concerned.

'Shall I help you clear up Miss?'

Wearily we collect dishcloths and tea towels to go in the twin tub. I'm too shaky to do the washing. It will have to wait until tomorrow. And I have to drive back to my bedsit in rush hour traffic.

Next day, it takes ages to prepare for school. My eyelashes have burnt off in the explosion and I've got burnt stubs instead of eyebrows. As for my hair, the front bit has frizzled away and it looks like I've been caught in a bomb blast. It's time to wear that pair of false eyelashes reserved for posh parties. Then paint black lash lines on my lower lids, just like Twiggy and I'll need to draw brown eyeliner curves for my missing eyebrows. At school there are some strange stares at my new look but I feel fine, if rather hairless.

Mr Shield has agreed to increase the amount of time Cynthia can work with me from five to ten hours a week. Each of the Science departments – Chemistry, Physics and Biology – have a full-time ancillary help and there are two full-time men dressed in brown overalls helping out in Woodwork and Metalwork. If he keeps sending more students to join my classes, I'm going to take him a tray of brandy snaps and a pot of tea to explain the importance of cookery lessons in the hierarchy of school education and how there are loads of jobs for people that know about food.

Now that Cynthia has more time she's had a clearout of my storeroom shelves. All the bloody Beryl Ware is stacked on my demonstration table.

Piles of pale pastel green plates, soup bowls, cups, saucers, teapots, milk jugs, sugar bowls, serving dishes with lids and gravy boats – all with the Beryl Ware mark on the bottom.

Why did She Who Ran Away buy so much stuff? We have enough crockery to serve breakfast, lunch and posh afternoon tea to all the teaching staff in this school. Mr Beryl and Mrs Ware must have made a pretty penny from selling their Mint Green, Iris Blue or Jasmine Yellow ranges. Sets of their crockery are found in schools, village halls, scout huts and hospitals around Britain and perhaps they will have some antique value one day.

'Cynthia – can we pack up most of this stuff and take it to the school flat. We won't be cooking for this many.'

The storeroom has more unwanted stuff – plain and frilly paper d'oyleys.

Nothing can be presented without a bloody d'oyley. It's plain for savoury things and frilly for sweet things.

So Cornish pasties, sausage rolls, cheese straws and savoury scones all get served on a plain d'oyley.

Fairy cakes, sweet scones, jam tarts, Eccles cakes and cream horns all need a frilly d'oyley.

If you bake a shepherd's pie, the dish must go on a plate with a plain d'oyley. For an apple pie, you serve it on a plate with a frilly d'oyley.

There are more rules for the round metal flan rings tied up with string on the storeroom hooks – plain for savoury and fluted for sweet. Rules, rules.

Half a mark off for the wrong flan ring or d'oyley. But is it doilie, doily or d'oyley? You decide.

Christmas cake

For days, pungent smells of cinnamon and nutmeg have wafted out of my cookery room as we mass produce mince pies for carol services and Christmas parties.

Marzipan fruits, coconut ice, chocolate truffles and Christmas logs are made for special gifts. Rich, dark fruit cakes have been stacked in my storeroom to mature and every week Cynthia helps me stick skewers into the cakes to dribble in brandy to add more flavour. This is not just any brandy. This is Hennessy finest cognac that Mark brought round to the front door of my bedsit house, but I didn't ask him to stay.

Now the cakes have been topped with marzipan and enrobed

in fondant icing and today we'll finish them with green holly leaves and blobby red berries moulded from the icing. Then we'll tie round the sides with a red ribbon in a giant bow. It's the modern TV look to keep up with fashion.

Vicky, as always, arrives late, dives into her bag and plonks a grubby Father Christmas and his grubbier sledge on top of her cake. The man, his reindeer and the sledge need a good scrub. She wraps a faded red tinsel band round the cake's middle and sticks a pin in to hold it in place.

'Our cake always looks like this and we have 'im on our cakes, Miss.'

Mr Shield the headmaster is invited to judge my Best Christmas Cake competition. This time, surely, he'll realise that I don't spend my lessons cooking my supper or doing my washing. He accused me of this a few weeks ago. He glances round the tidy cakes then makes his announcement.

'The winner is Vicky.' The room cheers. So the common looking Christmas cake decorated with a plastic toy wins. Vicky raises a fist in triumph. Some people have no taste.

That Friday, in the back section of the *Times Educational Supplement*, I read an advert for a job in Jamaica. Teaching Home Economics in Kingston on a two year contract with living expenses and accommodation included. I could save some money for a house deposit if ever I return to buy my own place. I've taught loads of children from Jamaican parents in my previous school and if the island is as charming as some of them, it will be fun.

I ring up the telephone number in the advert and ask them to send me an application form. Sunshine island with saltfish and ackee, welcome me. I'm meeting Mark with some friends for a drink tonight at The Flask in Highgate as I'm going home for Christmas. I'll thank him for the cognac and maybe share my plans for a two year Caribbean adventure.

My evening outings to The Loose Box have been successful and I've been on a few dates as part of my manhunt. The trouble is, we can't phone each other to fix or change a date since my bedsit has no phone. Dawn, the school secretary, is getting increasingly crabby taking personal calls for the young teachers who are working at the school. She does not want us in her office, however serious we say the call is. Being late for a date means I don't need to prop up some wall outside a busy pub and wait, looking like I'm a prostitute touting for business. There was one date when the man never came.

Now we're on to men with jobs beginning with C, I've met someone special. A Solicitor in the city. I know it begins with S but his name is James and fits the J target which is a long way off. And he's smartly suited and exceptionally handsome. Blue eyes and floppy blond hair and I like the way he's tall enough to look down at me when we talk. Our first date was on Saturday afternoon and we visited Marine Ices in Chalk Farm for the best Italian ice cream in London. For someone who seems so sophisticated, James is surprisingly unfamiliar with north London. We climbed up Primrose Hill and I gave him an impressive tour of the dramatic London landscape from the top. Views over to St Paul's Cathedral, The Post Office Tower and the giant skyscrapers in the city. It's a promising beginning and I really like the soft cashmere sweater he's wearing, which matches the colour of his eyes. We'll meet again when I get back to London after Christmas.

Peppermint creams

It's the last week before Christmas, and we're making peppermint creams as a Christmas present. More likely they'll eat them on the way home, or throw them at each other for target practice.

Gavin is back after another week's suspension. It's not clear what he's done, but some think that prison is his destiny.

I've been nervous about starting to educate Gavin again. Well not exactly again. I can't make any claim to have educated Gavin, ever.

'Hello everyone, and welcome to the peppermint cream lesson. Now you're ready, sieve your icing sugar into your bowls.'

Gavin lumbers down to my desk. He seems to have grown bigger.

'Miss, I'm making rum creams. Rum is for Christmas.'

He eyes me provocatively and sways unsteadily. I see he's grasping a small bottle of rum with most of its contents missing.

The room fills with sugary dust as the class shake their sieves. I stand up, ready for conflict.

'Gavin – get your cooking things ready and leave the rum on my desk.'

Amazingly Gavin puts the rum bottle on top of my marking and ties on his apron.

I face a class of surprised faces.

'Gather round – I'll show you how to crack an egg to separate out the white. Then mix it into the icing sugar with some peppermint essence and green colouring. OK let's start.'

Where's Gavin? I hope he's gone home. The rum bottle is still on my desk.

They sieve and mix and roll out balls of green dough. A sudden movement catches my eye. Gavin rises from behind his table and stamps his boots together. One of my pudding bowls is on his head and his right hand is raised in a Nazi salute.

'Miss. I told you. I am using rum.'

The group is silent. No one wants to be noticed by Gavin.

'Gavin – we can't use alcohol in the classroom. It's forbidden and you are under age for drinking.'

'You let them girls put brandy in Christmas cakes last week. Are you picking on me?'

Gavin puffs up like the Jolly Green Giant on those adverts for tins of sweetcorn. Only Gavin seems bigger.

And not jolly, green or friendly. And not singing 'Ho, Ho, Ho.'

He's right about the girls and their brandy.

But wrong that I would pick on him. Not in my cookery room with the door closed.

The group makes lines of peppermint creams in a kitchen silent with tension.

Gavin stumbles to my desk and grabs his rum.

I must deal with him or there will be trouble.

His great body thuds down in my chair and he lets out a noisy yawn.

'Gavin – the room's hot – you must be tired. Put your head down and rest.'

He spreads out his fleshy arms, and seems to doze. But Gavin can't be trusted – I wait for the storm.

The class quietly clears away. We smile together, wrap up the sweets in greaseproof paper and tie each bundle with a green ribbon. I send Len off to the office to get Mr James who comes in quietly and removes a dozy Gavin from my desk. Whew. That was easy. Perhaps he'll go to another school next term. And in a week it's the Christmas holidays.

Next day a packet is left on my desk.

'Hello Miss. I've moved into another group. I'll be in your O level class next term. Happy Christmas, Alice.'

I unwrap the red and gold paper. Inside is a tin of Yardley's English Lavender Talcum Powder. Now that brings back memories. Thankyou Alice. It's nice to be appreciated.

In the staffroom everyone says they're longing for Christmas. I'm not.

As soon as school closes, my Mini Traveller is packed with presents and my school Christmas cake. I'm ready to drive in sleeting rain, alone up the M1 to my parent's bungalow in Kettering. I'm dreading the holiday. And the questions.

The Christmas holidays

Whenever I go home there are always questions checking on my work and love life. Caring, kind but nosy questions that I don't like answering.

'How's the job going Jenny? Can you manage those naughty ones yet?'

'What's happened to Mark or has he gone for good?'

Several friends who stayed in Kettering have married, and one is expecting a baby. They like to remind me that at twenty four I am still on the shelf.

'You'd better not leave it too long.' warns Mary.

'All the best men are getting picked off. You'll stay a spinster if you hang about. It'll be like after the war. No men left.'

A shopping trip to Leicester market always cheers me up. The tented stalls are strung with shining light bulbs which brighten the dark afternoon of Christmas Eve.

Everywhere people scramble for late shopping – mounds of brussels sprouts, parsnips, carrots and soily potatoes clatter onto the scales to be weighed ready to feed the vast family gatherings. My mother, as usual, is searching for last minute bargains. Fresh foods that must be sold before the feasting begins.

The cheese stall has giant cylinders of local Stilton with delicate veins of blue mould. The stall owner pulls his cheese wire through the creamy curds, cuts us a huge chunk and wraps it in greaseproof paper.

On to the Melton Mowbray pork pie stall. My mother knows that the giant pies must be sold off as the market closes down for a week, so we are looking for a good deal. Our pie is so huge it could feed one of my classes and I suspect I'll get it served for breakfast and many other meals during my visit.

Next some Fenland celery, with its white, blanched stems covered in dark peaty Fen soil. This celery is only available in late winter and is so sweet and crunchy. We'll eat it with chunks of cheese, pie and buttered toast. Maybe one day someone will celebrate and value these foods from the Midlands – the cheese, the pies and the celery.

And don't forget the fabric stalls – there are rolls of soft woven wool which I'll rattle into maxi-skirts for cold winter outings and a roll of floral cotton will make a maxi-dress so I'll be all the rage and look like a prim country maid. A single maid.

We return to the stone coldness of the bungalow which my mother heats with wartime thriftiness. The ancient two bar electric fire only gets switched on to watch the TV and legs scorch if you stand too close.

Staying in my family home makes me sad. I am a visitor with a new London life, and a not very successful one. The rest of the holiday is a frenzy of sewing. In the spring sunshine I'll join the fashionable people parading my creations down the King's Road and wear the less outrageous outfits for school. So watch out Loose Box men. I'll return to my alphabet man-search and it's the letter C – Chefs or Cobblers might be a good start.

By New Year's Eve, the Melton Mowbray pie and Stilton cheese are nearly finished and I'm sick of celery. It's time to fill the Mini Traveller with my new clothes and head south to bright London lights, the welcome noise and the busyness. I'll miss the spring snowdrops, February catkins and pussy willow. But my bedsit life beckons and I'm ready to party.

Unlocking the front door I see a letter in Mark's handwriting on the hall table. The Kettering bungalow has no phone and it's impossible for anyone to ring me when I'm working at school. Dawn has issued more warnings to staff that she is not a messaging service for our private calls. Letters are one means of contact although I once got a telegram from Mark which was cycled round from the Kettering post office.

My shabby bedsit room is bungalow-cold and smells of damp. It's a freezing welcome to London as I read his note.

'Can I take you to dinner at San Lorenzo's in Knightsbridge next week? Christmas was awful. The family asked where you were. Ring me at work or leave a note on my car. You know where I live.x'

Offering me a restaurant meal, especially an expensive one, is like catching a crab with a piece of bacon, and best back bacon at that. I'll jump at the chance. But the kiss is not necessary if we are to stay friends.

I'll try and phone Mark from school at lunchtime and fix a date when Dawn leaves the office to go out for her break.

Spring Term 1973

The Little Nipper

There's a pile of crumpled foil under my desk so who's been into my room over the Christmas holidays? I unlock my drawer and there are more silvery bobbles and scrunched up blue and white paper along with a scattering of mouse droppings. My Christmas gift from teacher Pete was a bar of Fry's Chocolate Cream and it's been decimated. Hah. While the cat's away, the mice will play. The storeroom reveals more feasting. They've chewed off cardboard corners from packs of Scott's Porage Oats and mingled their poo with the oat flakes on the floor.

It's a job for caretaker Jim, so I leave him a note.

'Can you get me some Little Nipper Mouse Traps as the mice have set up the mouse café in my cookery room?'

I expect he's groaning at my return, but I must start my cooking lessons and need to be sure that the mice are not eating my food stores.

Scones are one of my favourite lessons and my class has gathered on the stools watching me rub the margarine into the flour and sugar.

It's staring at me, sitting on its haunches behind the back row of stools. Not bothered by my demonstration but ready to turn my lesson into classroom chaos.

'Look – the margarine rubs in until it looks like breadcrumbs.'

I hold up the bowl and make eye contact with the mouse.

'Class, just sit still for a minute.'

My grandmother has told me that you can frighten a mouse with a lot of noise.

The class senses my urgency as I scramble into the saucepan cupboard and emerge with the heaviest pans and largest lids.

'Bert.' I shush to him to come over as I hand him two lids.

'Liz. Quiet. Here.' She gets two pans. 'Bang you two. Make noise!'

'Follow me.' I set off to the back of the stools, banging my saucepan with a rolling pin.

It's working. My grandmother is right. The loud noise stops the mouse in its getaway tracks.

It's still, stunned by the spectacle of three people banging kitchen equipment.

But now what? How do I catch it? Kill it. Do what with it?

'Bert and Liz – keep banging – if it moves, catch it.'

I return with my mop bucket and invert it over the frightened mouse. It's trapped underneath but we can hear it scuttling and making an exit plan.

'Get the caretaker.'

I send timid Tim off to get Jim to rescue us. And just in case the mouse discovers how to escape from the bucket, I put my heavy catering tin of red jam on top to weigh it down.

'OK class, get on with your scones.'

The room hurries on but I can hear the mouse rattling its escape.

'Sieve flour onto the table, roll out and cut your scones then onto your tray and bake.'

Quick, quick. Don't ask for help. Quick, quick get rid of the mouse.

Help at last – it's Jim and Tim.

'Jim, there's a mouse under the bucket.'

I point to the jam tin.

He gives me a 'What am I supposed to do about that?' look.

I hand him Liz's saucepan and lid.

'Can you catch it in this saucepan and take it away? PLEASE.'

Jim is used to doing technical caretaking things like fixing locks and electrical switches. Mouse catching is not in his remit.

I mouth another 'PLEASE, so we can get on.'

He crouches, grabs the mouse and dumps it in the pan, thuds on the lid and leaves holding the pan out in front of him as if he's caught a bad smell.

The scones are ready and lined up on cooling racks. We'll eat them hot, spread with strawberry jam from the newly opened tin used for weighing down the mouse catching bucket.

I'll take Jim a plateful later when I collect my saucepan.

My application to work in Jamaica was posted last term and I worry that they might want a reference from my school and Mr Shield will ask why I'm leaving. But there's been no reply so I need to phone and chase it up.

That night Mark drives me in his new car to Knightsbridge. New car, new job he tells me. Must be a step up if this swanky vehicle is anything to go by. I wonder what his job title is. The waiters in San Lorenzo's make a great fuss shaking hands and with 'Ciao' and 'Bella' like they do to all their customers. It's a real treat to have my chair pulled out so I can sit down gracefully and I like the flourish when they shake my linen napkin out onto my lap. Mark selects an expensive bottle of Barolo and the waiter bows and congratulates him on his excellent choice. Excellent in adding to the price of the bill maybe. My meal is scrumptious – ravioli filled with ricotta, veal escalopes with fried sage leaves and creamy potatoes. We order tall glasses filled with warm Zabaione alla Marsala – this always reminds me of whisking eggs and sugar to a foam for my Swiss roll lessons. Then it's back to Hampstead and our separate homes.

Marmalade

Making marmalade is one of the kitchen joys of winter. How I wish someone would make a marmalade perfume to remind me all year of its citrusy fragrance.

A large box of Spanish Seville oranges has been left by the greengrocer outside my room and it's so cold as I wipe the January frost off their rinds. Giant aluminium preserving pans stacked high on the shelves in the storeroom are getting their first outing and they've been dusted, cleaned and scrubbed to remove the graveyard of spiders and flies who died inside unnoticed after years of neglect. Donated jam jars have been stripped of their labels and Cynthia has hidden the black haired golly stickers from pots of Robertson's Golden Shred in an envelope in my desk drawer.

'This is a lesson on Preservation. Work in groups and we'll share out the jars of marmalade at the end.'

Stroppy, foldy arms Carol looms towards me.

'I ain't sharing me cooking. How will I get a mark if we share?'

Carol and Vicky still randomly appear in this O level group when no other teacher wants them. The class despairs at their constant outbursts and I long for them to storm out to the station coffee bar.

'OK Carol – you and Vicky work as a pair. Now all of you, slice the orange peel really thinly like this.'

I cut tiny slivers of peel into thin strips which burst with zesty fragrance.

'Put the pith and pips in these pieces of muslin, tie up with string and drop in the pan to simmer with the squeezed orange juice and water.'

Cynthia has dusted down a bolt of white, soft muslin found on the top storeroom shelf. I imagine that She Who Ran Away used it to wrap round Christmas puddings ready for steaming or for straining milk curds to make cheese. But today my London teenagers are tying up bags with pips and pith to boil in our very large pans.

Carol shouts from behind her Formica table.

'We don't want no pips or peel or pith in ours. We don't eat them things.'

'Listen class – the pips and pith contain pectin which sets the marmalade, otherwise it's a runny syrup. And the orange peel is how marmalade should be.'

Carol scowls and mutters as the class settles into the gentle rhythm of slicing peel and squeezing juice.

Ugh. Now Vicky erupts and runs to the bin and spits out a vomit of orange flesh.

'Miss, this orange is vile. Sour as anything. It's off. We can't cook with them.'

'Class, put down your knives.' The quiet hush has been disrupted again.

'Seville oranges are bitter and sour. You don't eat them raw. You cook them with sugar. The first marmalade was made in a factory in Dundee. They got a delivery of these sour Seville oranges by mistake so they invented a new recipe – Dundee Marmalade made with sugar. Now let's get on.'

I feel like a perky, smartarse Brain of Britain contestant, only with a Midlands accent.

We tip vast quantities of Tate and Lyle sugar into the pans of simmering juice and the steam rises and blurs the windows. Ah! Bisto! The room smells delicious. A warm, pungent calm descends.

I spin round the pans sticking the jam thermometer into bubbling mixtures and Cynthia, my magical helper, follows with a cold plate for the wrinkle test.

'Don't lick your spoons or taste.'

The marmalade is reaching tongue scorching temperatures.

'If your marmalade wrinkles on this plate, it's setting.'

They look at me. Bewildered. Wrinkle? Why does it need to wrinkle?

We're ready. Hot jam jars fresh out of the oven are filled with a scalding, golden liquid. Quick now. Cover and seal it from germs with a circle of greaseproof paper and a crackly cellophane top tied with string.

The room glows orange – floaty slivers of finely cut peel dancing in the golden jelly of our east London marmalade.

Two pots are different. Carol and Vicky have abandoned their sugary syrup which will probably never set and definitely never deserve the name marmalade. They've no doubt gone for a smoke.

Cynthia is busy wiping sticky syrup from all the door handles, work surfaces and taps and I've got something to ask her before she leaves.

'Cynthia, when I went to Petticoat Lane Market on Sunday some men on the stall looked me up and down and said 'What a two and eight.' Is it a compliment?'

'Oh Jenny,' she laughs. 'It's Cockney rhyming slang for 'What a state.' I'm sorry but it's not nice.'

I'm going to do some homework on this Cockney stuff. There have been a few things said, like going for a Jimmy, that I don't quite understand.

To give me something to do in the evenings, I've enrolled for French conversation evening class at the Camden Institute which is a posh name for an Old Victorian school with grown up signs. The classroom doors offer Adult Education in just about anything from Maths O level to sewing for beginners. They are a lively group, gentle with my O level French attempts at asking for directions. We're all ages and a surprising number of men. Most want to get their French up to conversation level for their holidays. There's an empty seat next to Daniel, an attractive man with a deep, deep voice and a thick gold wedding ring on his left hand – a new trend for married men these days. He reminds me of Barry Gibb, the tallest of the Bee Gees, with a well trimmed beard and dark hair which curls down to his neck. When he turns the pages of his textbook or twists in his seat, there's a musky smell of patchouli oil. It's got an earthiness that I really like. At coffee break the class exit for the tea room, a dismal place down concrete steps past corridor walls painted council beige. Daniel walks in front. His shoulders are broad and he's tall. I like a man that's taller than me. Don't like doing the last waltz with a tiny man, slumped like a sack of potatoes over his shoulders. He buys me a plastic cup of coffee and we go outside for a smoke.

After class, I join the group at the nearby pub – they clearly get on well together. The group has decided that we will eat out in the local French restaurant and spend the night speaking French. I only hope the waiters are not London born Cockneys.

The mocks

It's the mock Home Economics exams in freezing January. Judgement time for me. And judgement time for them. In two hours they must spill out the knowledge that I have drilled into them over the past term. They may be able to cook two course meals and serve them with a flower arrangement, but if they don't pass this theory exam, all is lost. And I'm sure some of them struggle to read and write. Failure for them is failure for me. Results matter.

Mr Lewes comes into my room as I'm scrubbing down cake encrusted baking trays in the deep butler's sink. The twin tub is gurgling with a load of tea towels and dishcloths that I'll need to put into the spin dryer and then hang in the gas-fired dryers so they are ready for my afternoon class.

'Jenny – can you take the invigilation session this morning? The other teacher's not turned up.'

Bloody hell. It's not fair. I've longed for this free morning and a chance for some staffroom gossip and a smoke when I've done my chores. And now I'm going to be stuck in a freezing, dingy hall watching my classes as they struggle to answer the questions that I've set for their exams.

'You'll be on the stage and supervising the morning.'

Mr Lewes gives me a confident smile. Oh, that's great. No early warning to bring long johns and fingerless gloves for this freezing task. Instead I'm in my shortest mini skirt, skimpy rib top and white leather boots and will be perched on the stage above a group of bored teenagers.

I pick up work to mark and set off to the examination hall. As chief invigilator, I walk sternly past my chattering groups propped against the walls outside the hall.

'Hello Miss. It's a bit cold in there.'

'Thankyou Len, we'll have to manage.'

I prop open the double doors and march down the neat rows of hard chairs and splintery desks, which Jim the caretaker puts out especially for the exams. Their wooden tops are scratched with years of frustration.

Bill woz here. I hate Maths. Let me out.

And other fierce gouges too rude to mention made with a frustrated penknife or compass point.

Up the stairs to my position at another uncomfortable desk, centre stage. Brr.

'Open the doors, Mr Page, and let them in.'

The shambling queue idles down the aisles searching for their names. Cries reach me on the stage.

'Miss, I ain't got a ruler.'

'Miss, me pen won't work.'

'Miss, I need to go to the lav.'

I hand round spare emergency tools that I keep in my handbag, and let Len go to the toilet. It's time to start but several desks are still empty. The rowdy, naughtier boys have not turned up. Nor have Carol or Vicky. Some boys think exams are a waste of time – just messing about before real life begins. Carol and Vicky are no doubt thinking about babies. The pair should have studied Childcare, if Miss Rothwell had accepted them in her class.

'OK, it's time to start. You have two hours. No talking and you can't leave the hall until the time is up.'

'Ugh' groans Bert. 'This is the only exam I'm doing. I hate exams.'

'Turn your papers over, read all the questions first before you answer and please do your best.'

I want to add 'For me, please try.'

The ancient hall radiators ooze out little warmth on this freezing day. It's like sitting in a fridge. Mr Page paces up and down the rows and the metal studs on his boots clack soldier-like in the silence. Bert sharpens a pencil and coils of wood spiral down from his desk onto the parquet floor. I glower. My mouth commands 'Get on.' Bert continues his sharpening.

Suddenly the hall doors burst open. The missing girls explode into the hall.

Shouts of 'Miss, Sorry. Are we too late?' They are really hoping that I say 'Yes' so they can bunk off to the café.

Mr Page scowls and gives me a 'Shall we let the buggers in?' look. I nod and he raises his eyebrows in despair. The latecomers smirk their way to their seats, clatter down and rustle for writing tools. He mutters a desperate 'Get started.' and bangs some pens on their desks. For the next half hour boys and girls scribble away and a cold calm descends on the room. From my exposed perch I watch and wonder how I've taught them so many words that I will now have to mark over the weekend.

At a desk beneath me a handsome boy-man with dark floppy hair glances up. He's one of the sixth formers taking mock A level Maths. Bright boys don't choose my classes. They are siphoned off to study more useful subjects. The boy-man must be nineteen and he has the most startling grey-green eyes. Must be boredom to notice a boy's eyes. I pull my mini skirt hem down towards my knees and hope the ribbed top of my tights is not showing. His eye level is thigh level. The boy smiles and resumes his calculations. Pull yourself together. Stop dreaming. Handsome young boy-men who are four years younger must not be considered. I'm sad and single but I'm a teacher. If such thoughts become actions I'd lose my job and be in the *News of the World*.

Half an hour passes. Mr Page stops click clacking and leans despondently against the frame of the exit door. We'd both rather be drinking coffee and smoking in the staffroom than pacing this dreary place.

Some of the boys are stretching, packing their bags and yawning for attention. They mouth 'Miss.' 'Can we go?' 'Done.'

Mr Page slides over to the noisiest.

'Have you finished?' Yes. Yes.

'OK, go quietly and don't disturb the others.'

They lumber out, banging against the rows of desks and leaving the earnest behind. Time passes slowly. It's so cold. What are they writing about? There's no point dreaming of plans for my weekend. I'll be stuck in my bedsit with piles of marking. No wine bars or parties for me.

'Time's up, pens down.'

'Miss, I haven't finished ....'

'Too bad, pens down.'

I gather and stack the piles of answer papers as they file past, happy to be free.

Round the corner outside the hall the floppy haired man-boy or is he boy-man is bending down doing up his shoelaces.

He rises as I pass, towering over me and looking spectacularly beautiful.

'Hello Miss. Are you a new teacher? We haven't met before.'

'Yes. I mean no,' I reply. I almost want to shake his hand. 'Yes, I'm new here – just a term.'

If he was four years older we'd be the same age...don't be stupid. He's a student and you are the teacher.

He wanders off smiling, then glances round. His eyes are bright green in the winter light.

Cheeky boy. One day, when he's a man he'll break someone's heart. But it mustn't be mine.

James is meeting me in the queue at 7 o'clock outside the Hard Rock Cafe in Mayfair. This American style diner opened a year ago and I've heard it's so popular that the only way to get in without queuing is on the arm of a famous rock star. The rest of us just have to shiver outside as they don't take bookings. The line snakes down the busy street towards Hyde Park. I spot James immediately. He stands out above the rest – a taller, younger version of Robert Redford – and tonight he's mine. We won't need to speak. I'm just happy to gaze at his beautiful face, floppy hair and watch his eyes crinkle as he talks to me. It's like viewing the finest Van Gogh painting in the National Gallery. Gorgeous. But it's bloody cold in the queue. Thank god I wore the maxi skirt and velvet jacket I made over the holidays. We order burgers, chips and beers, only the tray of food that the waitress brings along doesn't look remotely like anything I've eaten in a Wimpy. My glossy bun is stacked high with a juicy burger, a slice from the biggest tomato ever, the crispiest lettuce and slivers of pickle all slathered in ketchup and mayonnaise. Held in place with a cocktail stick topped with an American flag. It's impossible to bite into without sauces dripping down my chin. And a paper cone of the crunchiest fries. Not the soggy chips wrapped in newspaper from the local chippie. The beer is so cold it makes my face freeze up. Nothing like the warm pub stuff. How I love this American food and this busy place. James, you have done us proud. After a passionate, if freezing hug we head off home – he goes west and I travel north. Ninety degrees difference on a compass – it seems too far. We'll meet up when I get back from half term. I've not told James about my Jamaican job application. There's something exquisitely, handsomely unattainable about him, but he'll do for now.

School dinners

Our school dinners are dismal, rushed affairs in a bleak dining room and the walls ooze smells of cabbage and chips. Students queue at the serving hatch to have food plopped onto faded plastic plates. They wolf it down at speed and rush out to meet their mates. Chips and baked beans are always on the menu and they smother their food choice in tomato ketchup, no doubt to add some taste.

My lunchtime meals have become grabbed snatches of bits from the storeroom and there's rarely time for a sit down school dinner. Now I live alone, money is tight and I'm still paying for the ingredients that I use in my demonstrations. I need to talk to Mr Shield about increasing my budget.

Dawn, the school secretary, visits my room.

'Jenny. A new rule says that if teachers supervise the school dinner room at lunchtime, they get a free meal – it'll save you money.'

Unions have won the recent battle that allows teachers to have time off at lunchtime and a free lunch will save me 50 pence a day. My school dinner ladies are kind and serve teachers the best food on a special table with a tablecloth and vase of flowers, so it's good value. But my room can't be left unsupervised if bread, quiches and cakes are cooking. I must stay until they are done, and my chance of a decent lunch is lost.

The main reason I avoid the dining hall is the menu choice. Battered Spam fritters are a menu favourite, served with chips and globby tinned spaghetti. I watch the cook open the large catering can of Spam, thump the end so the solid pink lump slides out and she cuts it into slices. At lunchtime each piece is dipped into batter then deep fried until crisp, just before the queues speed in.

She's told me that her food budget is really small but she feels really lucky that her school dinner ladies are so highly skilled. Their pastry making is legendary – sausage rolls with glossy puff pastry, cheese and onion pasties, meat pie with a crusty top and perfectly cooked egg and bacon quiches. Liver and onions is the least popular dish. We teachers behave like children and pick out the gristly tubes and line them up on the edge of our plates with lumps from the mashed potato. Friday's school dinner is the best but you need to be quick – the fish and chips with mushy peas soon runs out.

When it comes to puddings – or afters – the school dinner ladies enter stratospheric cooking heaven. Who can resist their treacle, apple or chocolate sponges served with thick custard? Or the steamed jam roly poly made with suet crust pastry, apple crumbles and jam tarts. These ladies are accomplished cooks and they could teach me a trick or two.

In exchange for my free meal, I must supervise students in the dining hall. We must check that they clear away their plastic plates and scrape uneaten waste into the pig bin as the room is transformed back into a classroom after we've eaten. Tables and chairs are wiped down and stacked, chunks of uneaten sausage roll and squashed chips swept away, while the hard working school cooks clatter and clean, leaving the school kitchen spotless for the next day.

So, no thank you. I won't be swapping my lunch hour for a free meal and supervision. And one day, maybe someone will come along and change things for the better.

Dawn returns with a folded piece of paper.

'Jenny, I forgot. Someone called Mark rang the school and said can you call him today.'

She hands over the folded note and I feel she wants to add 'Please.'

At the end of the school day I visit the secretary's office and ring the number inside the paper. Yes, let's meet tonight at Jack Straw's Castle. Dawn pretends she's not listening but she's smiling at something.

Black leg

My local rep is holding a NUT meeting in the Town Hall. For months there have been rumblings of discontent. Teachers are disillusioned with pay and working conditions and want change. I squeeze into the back of the gloomy hall. There are no spare seats and people are jammed together. The fat man on the stage thumps his fist on the table and rallies us to take strike action. All NUT members must come out. 'Ra! Ra!' they chant.

When I started teaching, I'm told to join a union, to support me in difficult times and help me get a fair deal. I sign up and pay my dues, unaware that I have a choice. Now, in the news, there are plans for widespread strike action. Is it going to be like the TV comedy 'The Rag Trade' where Miriam Karlin shouts the catchphrase 'Everybody Out!'?

We get a memo when the strike is planned.

'On strike day, the school will stay open for teachers who do not belong to unions or have joined professional bodies and those who are not striking. Students are not allowed into school as there will be no supervision.'

The staffroom bustles with placard making and banners ready for the march.

I don't want to go. If I strike I lose my pay for the day, which I can't afford to do. But deep inside I can't do it. I don't want to march on Parliament. Surely change can be effected without this thumping, shouting and marching? I tell the union rep that I'm coming into school. He looks bewildered and cross.

Then things get nasty.

As I'm taking a class, someone thumps on my classroom window and shouts 'Scab.' The group turns to me for a reaction. I'm shocked, ashamed and voiceless at this angry protest. Things get nastier. More bangs on my classroom window, this time it's 'Blackleg.'

The union rep sees me at the end of the school day.

'Jenny, I suggest you follow the rest of us.'

On strike day I come to school.

I'm dragging wet tea towels and dishcloths out of the spin dryer when Len comes into my room.

'Len, you're not supposed to be in school. Students stay at home today.'

'Shall I make us a cup of rosy lee, Miss?'

I know he's teasing me with Cockney rhyming slang and perhaps he'll share some more words. It's just the two of us and I've no lessons and no friends in the staffroom.

Len busies himself putting the kettle on and searching for cups, saucers, a milk jug and a teapot. The atmosphere is sad. Len seems sad, and I'm sad. He puts the teabags into the warmed teapot and leaves it to brew, then gathers an armful of wet dishcloths and hangs them on the bars of my gas-fired dryer.

Len sometimes stays behind and helps me clear up and never takes his cooking home. I wonder if, like me, there is no-one there to welcome Len after school. Somehow it feels like Len and I have things in common and we offer each other wordless support. What will happen when he leaves school at Easter as he's sixteen, barely able to read and write and with no qualifications?

Len pours the tea and stirs three large spoonfuls of sugar into his cup and we sit and drink together. No words. Just thoughts. 'Len – I've been doing a bit of Cockney writing for my homework – can I read it to you?'

He looks up, puzzled.

'OK – see if you can understand what I've written. 'There was this man who went to the bathroom for a jimmy, then had a butcher's in the mirror and brushed his barnet. He came down the apples and pears, sat down and switched on the custard then the dog and bone rang to ask where was his Duke of Kent so he got in the jam jar and took the man a ton.'

'Did you understand it, Len?' He's bewildered.

'Let me explain what it means. Jimmy stands for jimmy riddle – piddle, butchers comes from butcher's hook – look, barnet stands for Barnet fair – hair, apples and pears – stairs, custard stands for custard and jelly – telly, dog and bone – phone, Duke of Kent – rent, jam jar – car, and a ton is £100.

So. There was this man who went to the bathroom for a piddle, then had a look in the mirror and brushed his hair. He came down the stairs, sat down and switched on the telly then the phone rang to ask where his rent was, so he got in the car and took the man £100. Do you think I'm going to be able to speak Cockney Len?'

He's baffled. 'Miss, you know that jumper you wore for that staff hockey match? It said Bristol University on the front. You do know that Bristol means Bristol City and in Cockney that means titties? You went to a university for tits. And that's why they all laughed.'

Thanks, Len for reminding me of a deeply embarrassing moment when I definitely didn't understand the cultural references of the watching crowd. And thanks Cynthia for explaining about the time in the market when the men said I looked a state.

On TV that night I see the marches from Trafalgar Square, waving banners and placards and then fighting starts as strikers and police come face to face. What will my days be like if I don't protest with the majority? It's a worry for my future. The next day in the staffroom, they're very excited.

'Did you see me knock off the policeman's helmet?'

It's Lynn who only last week invited me round for tea in her lovely family home.

The next time the union calls us out, I'll join the strike and won't go into school. Money will be deducted from my wages and I'll spend the day wandering around Hampstead Heath, far away from this mess. It is time to leave the union, and maybe time for me to leave London and have a complete change.

And what's happened to my job application for Jamaica? They are being really slow at responding.

Swiss rolls

The minute Mr Shield agreed to more funds I ordered new electric beaters and now they've arrived I'm going to teach a lesson on time saving gadgets. The famous TV cook Marguerite Patten has written a book called *500 recipes for Electric Mixers and Blenders*, and this is her Introduction:

'I have tried to convince many people that mixers save time, trouble and money as well as enabling you to prepare dishes that normally could be too complicated for a busy housewife.'

More books that expect housewives to do everything, but I'm teaching boys.

Marguerite has some tasty recipe ideas for my lessons on wretched invalid cooking – Liver soufflé made from liver, white sauce and eggs. Can't wait to try that out. And her fruit fools have gone posh – now it is Gooseberry foule with green colouring. Has Marguerite joined the Fanny Cradock fan club and copied her way of calling dishes by French names?

They've gathered ready to cook.

'Have you got lots of Valentine cards today, Miss?'

It's nosy Carol. Why are they so obsessed with my private life?

'Class – we need to get on, so no more questions about my private life, Carol. Today we're making Swiss roll. You're doing a speed test to see if the new electric beaters can beat the rotary beaters, wire balloon whisks and forks.'

Swiss rolls can take ages to whisk, cook and roll up. The preparation time is in proportion to the tasteless, dry cake that you get at the end. Corner shops sell tiny Cadbury's Swiss rolls, coated in chocolate and filled with buttercream, which are much better than anything I can cook.

But a Swiss roll is a high level, much admired cooking skill revered by EXAMINERS. Get it wrong and you've got a flat, dry biscuit. Get it right and you get a dry, spongy cake.

You only need four ingredients to make a Swiss roll – eggs, sugar, flour and jam and since these emergency rations can come from my storeroom, everyone can join in.

If they don't want the cake, I'll sell it to the highest bidder in the staffroom. There are dozens of Swiss roll tins stacked in the storeroom, so She Who Ran Away must have been managing some sort of cake factory.

Whisking eggs and sugar is our first task.

Gavin thunders in late and I point him to an empty stool. By some cookery magic he sits down.

'Crack the eggs into the bowl with the sugar, put the bowl over a saucepan of hot water and whisk until thick.'

Like the best Blue Peter demonstration, I've done one earlier. If only I had some marsala it would make Zabaglione instead of dry old Swiss roll.

'The eggs leave a trail when ready and you can write some letters with it. Cynthia is going to choose who gets which whisk and you write down how long it takes to get creamy and drip like this.'

I hold up the whisk and let the thick mixture drip down to make a swirl. I long to write something rude.

Cynthia hands out the whisks. She knows who to choose for each type and I've just whispered 'Give Gavin a fork.'

She knows the rules for this whisking test – misbehave and you get the wire whisk = some of the boys.

Have the occasional shouty session and you get the rotary whisk = some boys and a few girls.

Well behaved and you can plug in my new electric beaters = keen students like Alice and Len, my favourites.

Some of my lessons are like training dogs. Behave and you get treats. Mess around and don't follow instructions and it's going to be tough for both of us.

'OK let's start whisking.'

The room hums with competitive beating and Cynthia and I wander round inspecting foamy trails.

'When it's ready you can write letters in it.'

Alice, Len and the quiet girls are done. Bert and Gavin are furiously beating.

Gavin looms over to a boy with a rotary whisk and swaps it with his fork.

'Gavin – that's not a fair test. You can't change whisking tools during foamy beating.'

He scowls and I abandon his dog training for now.

'Class – fold in the flour with a FIGURE OF EIGHT using a metal spoon. Gently so that you don't knock out the air.'

The figure of eight folding process is one of the hallowed techniques in cake making.

'Now spoon it into the tin and bake.'

Swiss roll is quicker to cook than to make, but once it's done all hell breaks out to turn it from flat cake to its rolled up finish.

'Tip out onto the sugared tea towel. Quick, while it is hot. Cut off the sponge edges, spread with jam then ROLL AND HOLD.'

I am the sergeant major marching round the class as they cut, spread then push the cake uphill over the jam.

'HOLD. Do not look at it yet.'

'OK, undo the tea towels.'

It's like taking off the blindfold at a hide and seek party. Their worktables fill with a dazzling array of golden Swiss rolls, dusted with caster sugar and oozing red jam.

'Onto a frilly d'oyley for marking please. And Alice won the beating race.'

This dry, fatless sponge only keeps its freshness for a few hours so it needs eating quickly. The boys shuffle off taking huge spongy bites with rings of sugary crystals sticking to their lips.

Cynthia brings me a cup of tea and we sit down and cut two slices from a very nice Swiss roll that someone has left behind.

'Did you get a Valentine card today, Jenny? My husband has sent me one every year since we met at school.'

I left my bedsit long before the post arrived and didn't send any. My grandmother said 'You have to give to receive' so I reckon my luck is out.

There are three envelopes addressed to me on the hall table in my bedsit house when I get back. Two are Valentine cards – one from Mark and the other from James. Well, well.

The third is the long awaited letter.

'Please come for a preliminary interview for the role of Home Economics Teacher in Kingston, Jamaica.'

Thank god it's in half term so I can attend in my own time and my school won't know about my escape plan.

Vicky

Vicky has been subdued since the start of term and is not turning up for lessons or palling up with Carol so often. And I haven't seen her sidle up to Len and stroke his back like she used to. But I'm thankful that she's stopped asking about my love life and future wedding plans. I don't need reminders of my extended spinsterhood.

'Vicky, are you cooking today? I've got some ingredients in the storeroom. You can make some jam tarts.'

'No Miss, I feel sick.'

She lays her head on the cooking table.

'Read this chapter on Planning Meals and answer the questions. I'll see you at the end of the lesson. Sit at my desk, out of the way.'

I hand over the textbook, a biro and some paper. Boring, boring work. I wonder if she'll bother.

Today we're making quiches and it's a busy lesson. Cynthia joins me as we check that their shortcrust pastry ends up as a dough ball and not a floury glue that sticks to the tables. Next, the tricky task of easing the pastry into the flan rings, to make the pastry case.

'No holes in your pastry else your filling will run out.'

Bake it blind, make the egg and bacon custard, put it back in the oven and Voila. A golden, set custard with a crumbly pastry. They've done well.

As the class packs away, Vicky edges to the door.

'Vicky, can you wait for a minute. You've not taken part in lessons for ages. What's happened?'

'I told you I'm sick, Miss.'

'You were sick last week. Did you go to the school nurse or see your doctor?'

She winces at the suggestion.

'They can't do nothin'.'

My brain goes Ping. I have the answer. Of course the school nurse and her doctor can't do nothin'.

Headstrong, exasperating, gossipy Vicky is fifteen, desperate to leave school and become a hairdresser. And now some of her wishes may come true. Len has joined his mates and is edging out the door. No glance back. No recognition. If she's pregnant she probably won't come to school, and may spend weeks in the unmarried mother's house a long way from here. She might have to give birth in a faraway place and be told it will be best for her baby to be adopted. They'll no doubt teach her to cook but she won't take any exams and she can't come back to this school. For now I suspect Vicky's dreams of becoming a hairdresser may have been shattered.

Macaroni cheese

The usual line of boys who squabble, jostle and push each other into the wall outside my cookery room is missing. The boys have frightened off most of the girls who have either moved to another of my classes or changed to another subject. Some days I would like to strip off my nylon overall, throw my rubber gloves in the bin, lock my door, and sit in my Mini Traveller in the car park rather than teach this class.

But today, only Len and Sam are propped outside my door. Once inside we face the pile of ingredients for macaroni cheese and baked apples. How to use all of this food with just two students? The cheese is cut into equal sized chunks, and the greengrocer has brought identical cooking apples.

'Hello boys – it looks like you'll get larger portions today. Where are the others? Are they bunking off?'

Neither boy replies.

'You can have two apples each as the others are missing.'

They'll loosen up if we start cooking.

We core the apples and push sultanas, raisins and mixed spice into the centre, top with a knob of margarine and into the oven to bake. Quiet. Something serious has happened. Not even a knob joke today.

There are lots of excuses when students miss lessons. Doctor's or dentist's appointments are popular.

Walthamstow dog track is down the road and betting is a profitable pastime. Boys mess about in Maths lessons as they see no point in Pythagoras' theorem but they can calculate the outcome of an each way bet as quickly as they say yep to one of my lemon curd tarts.

'So have they gone to the dogs or is it the horses today?'

Silence. Len stirs the boiling macaroni.

We whisk a white sauce by the all-in-one method invented by Stork margarine. Milk, marg and flour into the saucepan then whisk and heat until it thickens. Easy.

'Bring your saucepans to the dem table and we'll finish the cheese sauce together. A bit of extra cheese today.'

Still not a word.

'Season with Colman's mustard powder, pepper and a little Worcestershire sauce and taste it.'

Delicious – we like tasting.

'Mix the sauce into your macaroni with some frozen peas.'

The room feels warm and cosy. They must crack soon.

'Come on Len – tell me where they are.'

He shrugs.

'Most of them have gone to court, Miss.'

'Why's that Len? You can tell me.'

Sam winces. He's not happy with Len giving away secrets. And I reckon Len has other stuff he's not sharing about Vicky.

'Neil and Tom got caught after they broke into a factory.'

Len grins.

'Tom dropped his gloves after he'd climbed through a window. They had his name in.'

We chuckle together. A boy burglar with gloves labelled with his name – his mum should have attached them with elastic that went round his neck and down his sleeves so they didn't get lost.

'And the others?'

'Alan borrowed a milk float. The milkman left the keys in and Alan thought it was a quick way to get to school. But the man ran after and caught him then called the police.'

Roast chicken, dozy Alan, always late, so this spontaneous act is a surprise.

'And John? Where is John?'

'John got caught for driving too fast and it wasn't his car.'

And he's fifteen.

The list of petty thieving, borrowing bikes and cars and general mischief goes on. The consequences could be serious – a fine, probation or worse still they could be sent away to a young offenders institution and Borstal.

We pile the macaroni into foil dishes, grate more cheese on top, decorate with slices of tomato and a sprig of parsley, then wrap them with instructions to heat in the oven with the baked apples for 30 minutes ready for their tea when they get home. Len wants to leave his in my fridge till tomorrow lunchtime. He doesn't take things home.

This quiet, gentle afternoon with no jokes or challenges feels rather sad. What will the future hold? Will my class shrink to two?

Tonight I'm meeting James to see a film together. 'Last Tango in Paris' is showing in a tiny cinema just off Leicester Square. It's a drab, dingy place for a date – a bit of a dive, and I'm surprised that smartly dressed James would want to sit in these mucky cinema seats. It feels like the sort of place that old men visit in the afternoon wearing their beige, stained, buttoned up raincoats before they skulk off to Soho for more serious deeds. Marlon Brando and that woman spend most of their time writhing around naked. And the film is so rude. I wonder if James is giving me a hidden message but he's made no moves so far. The Paris street scenes bring back happy memories of holidays with Mark with his fluent French which was so impressive when he ordered a meal or hailed a taxi. There's something about James that feels a bit skanky. I tell him I've got to get back for an early start.

Spring Half Term 1973

The slop pot

Spring half term means a return to Kettering. It avoids spending bleak bedsit days alone and I know that Northamptonshire, Rose of the Shires, is springing into life. There'll be walks in the aconite woods and time to catch the last snowdrops, and our usual trip to Leicester market to stock up on new fabrics and the bargain fashion rejects from the local textiles factories. They take the labels out but I've seen this stuff in the fashionable boutiques in Kensington High Street and the King's Road.

My mother is desperate to show me her new toy – her slow cooker.

'You'll like this modern gadget, you with your new ideas. I just plug it in and leave it on all day and it cooks our meals over a light bulb. It really saves money – you should buy one.'

That week, after several light-bulb-cooked stews, we sit down to evening meals with dread. The slow cooker is secretly renamed the slop pot. Mother slops in ingredients in the morning, switches on the light bulb, leaves it on all day and slops it out at night. As my holiday progresses, the slop pot stores a magic brew of reused food.

'You don't waste anything – just add food to the pot.'

It is no surprise when lumps of Sunday's roast lamb appear in Tuesday's stew along with bits of roast potato and Brussels sprouts. Once, in a hurry to get to Leicester market, she emptied in some frozen carrot chunks. The light bulb does its best at defrosting, but we meekly eat frozen chunks that night.

'Never mind', she says. 'I can heat it up properly for tomorrow.'

I wonder why she never sits to eat with us but she wants no criticism of her cooking. Once when I said the stewed beef was too tough to chew, she banged down her cooking tools and stomped off to her sewing room.

'You cook next time.' When I tried it was met with 'Mucking up good food.'

Slow cookers are becoming the rage with more women going out to work. In the thrifty 1970s, it's important to learn about saving fuel costs. I'll ask Mr Shield for some money to buy one for school.

Her other new toy is a large chest freezer. On my Christmas visit, the top opening lid barely shut as it was stuffed with frozen fruit and vegetables from her garden and packs of Sainsbury's reduced food with their yellow stickers.

Since the arrival of the chest freezer, my mother has stopped serving seasonal vegetables and heats up mystery frozen choices instead. The bags are unlabelled and have unidentifiable contents which have frosted into obscurity. Runner beans, spinach and carrots are served all year round but never taste like the ones picked fresh from her garden. The thrill of opening a plastic tub containing a rare treat of Wall's Vanilla Ice Cream is dashed as it's more likely to be full of frozen plums, raspberries and blackberries or leftover stew.

I post her a *Home Freezing Handbook* when I get back to London so she can learn how to bag, label and date her frozen stuff. A pair of step ladders might be more useful so she can climb into the freezer and turf it all out. And I'll add a chest freezer to my list of things I want for school. We'll fill it with useful cooking bits like frozen peas to add to quiches and macaroni cheese and freeze loaves of sliced bread to make cheese toasties.

My Jamaican interview is looming on Friday, so I head back ready for the challenge.

Jamaica

How can I find out more about Jamaica before my interview? What about asking someone on the fruit and vegetable stall in Camden street market? The man who works there has long, twisted dreadlocks which fan out from his multicoloured Jamaican rasta hat. His stall is piled with huge green plantains, sweet potatoes and yams and sometimes there are limes and green mangoes which he slices and offers from the point of his knife. He told me that the large round green things that he sometimes sells are breadfruits and the trees were planted on the island to feed the slaves. In winter I've bought maroon, spiky sorrel flowers to make a bright red Christmas drink with lots of sugar. In summertime the stall is jolly with Jamaican music and he brings out a sugar cane crushing machine that oozes sweet juice into a glass full of ice cubes.

He's there with friends, sitting on stools by the stall and it's February cold.

'Excuse me, gentlemen. I've got an interview for a job in Jamaica and I wondered if any of you know about the island?'

The sun shines out of their smiles.

'Jamaica, beautiful island. Sandy beaches, blue seas.'

'We grab mangoes and avocados from the trees on the way to school.'

'Red snapper and king crabs.'

'And coconuts fall on me head.'

'It's hot, not like here.'

They pretend to shiver inside their overcoats.

'Where is the job?'

'In a college in Kingston.'

'Ah, lady. Kingston is dangerous. Guns and gangs and things. You don't wanna go there. That's why we're here in freezing England.' They shiver and shake their heads at my plans.

'It ain't safe like Camden.' They chuckle between themselves.

The ladies at my interview are polite and smiley. What do I know about the island? Am I willing to stay there for two years? No-one special that I'm leaving behind? No family that are important? I'm twenty four – am I a bit young for the job? Have I taught Jamaican children before?

They've got other people to interview in the coming weeks as it's a popular job, but they think I'm a good candidate and will write and tell me if I'm to be called for a second interview.

Pancakes

Pancakes are a lesson firmly on my school calendar. Shrove Tuesday changes with the date for Easter and we know when it is coming as plastic, yellow, squeezable Jif lemons appear in the shops and the TV advert reminds us 'Don't forget the pancakes on Jif Lemon Day.'

As a child, on pancake day my mother became my pancake servant. She'd stand by the gas stove and toss as many pancakes as I could eat. I'd finish one while the next was turning golden in the pan. Up to ten pancakes were fried until crisp, tossed, folded into quarters, sprinkled with caster sugar and squeezed with fresh lemon juice – an expensive treat. No Jif lemon. That's not real. It's muck.

It's been two weeks since the boys went to court and I sit at my desk and watch to see who turns up. Neil and Tom come in first, perky as always. They dump their bags and pile duffle coats on top then tie on their aprons. Alan and John arrive with other latecomers and soon the room is noisy and bustling.

'What are we cooking today, Miss? I'm hungry.'

The room will return to its afternoon chaos and I am pleased.

'We're making pancakes today. It's Shrove Tuesday.'

You need a frying pan that does not stick to make really good pancakes and She Who Ran Away may have left me cupboards full of crusty cake tins, but there's a stack of ready proved, very used frying pans in my storeroom that are perfect for pancakes.

'Class, Shrove Tuesday is the last day for rich foods to be eaten before Lent. Eggs and milk were rich foods for many people so that's why we're making pancakes.'

Silence. They've got bowls of beaten pancake batter waiting.

It's time for me to demonstrate my tossing skills.

'Melt a knob of lard in the pan until it has a smoky blue haze, pour in a thin layer of batter and swirl around.'

Smirks. OK. It's knobs again. Bert, please don't ask the size of a knob.

The lard melts and smokes, the batter sizzles, and a thin pancake crispens, bubbling with little golden craters, ready for tossing.

'You need to practice tossing. The first pancake often doesn't toss easily.'

'Tom's a good tosser, Miss. Get him to show you how he does it.' Bert is sparky today.

Sniggers and nudges then Tom lifts his hand and bats Bert round the head.

'Is your boyfriend good at tossing, Miss?' It's Carol. Arghgh!

I want to tell her I have no boyfriend. That Sandy woman saw to that. And where is Vicky today?

This lesson is descending into chaos and cookery terms have become playful banter.

'Look. Just throw your pancakes in the air so they flip and land upside down.'

It would be much easier to say toss.

The room busies with frying pancakes and there's a loud round of applause and shouts when one lands back in the pan after it has somersaulted through the air. Some boys toss high for a double flip and I suspect the pancakes that drop on the floor are deliberately enhancing the game to increase the laughter. Carol enjoys the fun but most of the girls flip their pancakes safely and neatly with a palette knife.

They're ready for eating. Quickly. No time to remove aprons or put out tablecloths. Pancakes must be hot, rolled up or folded with a sprinkle of sugar and a squirt of lemon juice. The plastic Jif ones from the corner shop have to do. No pips or bother on Jif Lemon Day.

The boys push in mouthfuls, rinse their plates and charge out to their next class.

The letter on the hall table in my bedsit house has a typed address label. I've been shortlisted for the Jamaican job and can I come for a further interview?

I need to get advice from Mark. Is Jamaica as dangerous as the market men suggest? The drinks company that he works for has contacts all over the world. A lot of rum is drunk in Jamaica so he could get in touch with the main rum distillery and check for my safety. He's in when I ring the doorbell of our old flat but I don't go inside when he answers the door. He seems rather shocked at my Caribbean plans but promises to check and get back to me.

Rhubarb rhubarb

It's the weekend. I'm back in Kettering and visiting my grandmother to get some free rhubarb from her garden for my lessons. The pink, tender stems that she forces under metal buckets are saved for the family but she's happy for me to pick the huge clumps thriving on her compost heap.

I cut armfuls – leaves and all – but Grandma's bothered.

'Those rhubarb leaves can poison people.'

She's heard a story of someone who ate the leaves, had severe stomach pains and ended up in hospital. Grandma boils the leaves with water to make her aluminium pans shiny clean and she reckons that if the leaves strip your stomach in the same way as they remove stuck bits from her pans, then that could be painful.

'Don't give those children the leaves. You could get into trouble.'

'Don't worry – I'll warn them.'

Grandma knows about London children. Evacuees from east London were billeted in her house during the Second World War. They attended Park Road Infants School, thrived on her cooking and helped with her garden. She's very proud of her certificate from Queen Elizabeth II thanking her for this service, which she keeps in a faded envelope with its official stamp in her treasured front room cabinet.

'Just a word. Have you got another boyfriend yet? Time's passing Jenny. This job is not everything you know. Make time to watch the flowers grow.'

Bah. I'm twenty four, everyone is getting married, I live alone in a dismal Hampstead bedsit and drive an old Mini Traveller with green moss, which matches the colour of the car's paintwork, growing on its window edges. And I have a job where most of the time I'm dressed in a nylon overall and matching pink rubber gloves, and I rarely leave the room. Time is passing. And I return back to London to try harder.

When I leave the bedsit in the morning I find a note under my car windscreen wiper. Mark has news on Jamaica. He'll wait in the Holly Bush pub tonight at eight for a drink. I've got a busy day today as I'm taking the class out on a trip but Mark's advice is really valuable so I'll be there.

Back in the classroom, I plonk the pile of rhubarb on the demonstration table.

'Class – to warn you – these leaves are poisonous, so don't eat them. They can give you a stomach ache and some people have died after eating them.'

Who knows if the death story is true? I have their attention.

'How did they die?' It's early but Bert is alert.

'The leaves contain toxic oxalic acid and that means they are poisonous.'

'Why does the poison just go into the leaf? What about the rest?'

Bert has a clever point. I'll have to ask the biology teacher.

'Miss, can I have those leaves?'

Ah ha. I can see where this diversion is leading. Bert's after my rhubarb leaf mountain. We've just had the school acid attack in the Chemistry lab when a boy was pushed onto a stool covered in nitric acid. It burnt the backside off his school trousers and he was whipped off to Whipps Cross Hospital to have the skin on his bottom soothed. Whispers said Gavin was involved. He was supposed to be going to another school, but it turns out no one will have him, so he could be back in my lessons.

Next to enter the school gossip calendar could be the rhubarb poisoning scandal. And it'll be my fault.

'Bert, I'm taking these leaves home, so just watch my demonstration on Rhubarb fool that we're making today and stop plotting. Remove the leaves, wash and chop the stems, put them in a saucepan and cook in a little water with the lid on until they are soft.'

I'm learning to give my classes very clear cooking instructions after several disasters ended in the bin. I once told Robert to boil his potatoes until they were soft so he stuffed them, unpeeled, into my electric kettle, filled it with water and clicked it on. It took ages to poke out the mushy, mashed up bits.

For today's lesson I've got a 'Here's-one-I-made-earlier' bowl of Grandma's pink, cooked rhubarb just like a Blue Peter presenter. It gets passed round the group with little approval.

'Now to make custard.'

My grandmother and I used to make Bird's custard together to go with her apple crumbles, gooseberry pies and strawberry jam sponges. There is a magic moment when you stir pale peach custard powder with gritty granulated sugar and mix with a little milk. Suddenly the mixture turns into a bright yellow liquid – a chemical mystery that probably holds its truth in tartrazine.

'To make the custard, pour hot milk into this mixture and stir quickly until it thickens.'

A golden, glossy custard glimmers in the bowl.

'Mix together your cooked rhubarb, the custard and some drops of red colouring.'

The red colouring is made from crushed cochineal beetles but I'm not sharing that secret. Imagine the screams.

'We ain't eating beetles.'

'Whisk the egg whites until stiff and fold in. Spoon into a glass dish and top with a glacé cherry.'

They chop, cook and stir, beat and mix. Soon my table is covered with glass dishes in various shades of pink. Each served on a saucer with a frilly d'oyley. Always a bloody d'oyley. There are hundreds to use in the storeroom.

The lesson is over and we have made a potion of rhubarb with enhanced colours and flavours which richly deserves the name fool. I must ask Cynthia what happened to the rhubarb leaves.

The Holly Bush is one of the oldest and cosiest pubs in Hampstead and Mark takes our drinks to a quiet table by the roaring fire. This is a snug and comfortable place to meet for a chat on a chilly night.

'Jenny, I've spoken to the distillery in Jamaica and they are very concerned about your plans to go alone to Kingston. The city has a lot of unrest, and things are not safe at the moment. Especially for a young, single female. Anyway, I don't want you to leave.'

Mark is nice, kind and seems rather sad. I thank him and decide I'm going to write and tell them that I've changed my mind and don't want the Jamaican job after all. He smiles hopefully. He's attractive enough for another Sandy to be lurking somewhere. But he's lost my trust for now and I'm not telling him that I've been seeing the handsome alternative, James, who has invited me down to the country to meet his parents at the weekend.

Dinner à deux

Some of my students have come with me to the Hotel and Catering Exhibition at London's Olympia and I'm hoping to show them the range of jobs they could choose in the food industry. Many stalls have samples of readymade dishes for hotels, restaurants and wine bars and I particularly love a range of French frozen ready meals. Country paté in tiny, brown earthenware pots, Duck a l'Orange topped with glazed orange slices and real chocolate mousse made with proper chocolate, not the cheap cooking chocolate that we use in school. All you need is a fridge and freezer to run a restaurant. No need for a chef. I doubt this ready-made food will catch on but the food we tried tasted delicious.

It was a strange visit to James' parents home. A journey down to the suburbs on a Saturday was not my idea of a trip to the country. And their 1930s semi was not the kind of house I had expected. James seemed posh enough for his parents to have a large detached property set in extensive grounds. Why had he brought me here when we barely knew each other? Mrs James was dumpy and kind as she sat me down on a plump, soft settee in her net curtained lounge. She bustled into the kitchen and returned proudly wheeling a shiny hostess trolley laden with food. The top tier had a plate of assorted sandwiches, crusts removed, cut into wedges, decorated with two halves of tomato lilies and sprinkled with mustard and cress. Next was a pile of perfectly baked fruit scones cut with a fluted cutter, a saucer of butter curls and a dish of dark red jam, which no doubt Mrs James had made herself. Underneath, the cake tier – Victoria sponge, slices of buttered tea bread and ginger parkin. Marguerite Patten would be proud. The bottom tier was the final triumph – a large cut glass bowl filled with an enormous trifle decorated with perfect swirls of whipped cream topped with glacé cherries, angelica diamonds and sprinkled with slivers of toasted almonds. And a meringue topped pastry dish that I so hoped was lemon meringue pie. Mrs James would pass my exams with full marks and she could get a job in the Ritz tea room if she ever stopped being a housewife.

James and Mrs James disappeared into the kitchen to fetch out trays laden with tea serving stuff. They were replaced by a lively golden coloured boxer dog who nosed between my legs then chomped into the custard and piped cream from the trifle and slathered out a chunk of the pie. Which was definitely lemon meringue now that he had exposed the filling.

James returned with his mother and we sat politely drinking tea from her best china cups. There was no mention of their badly behaved, unhygienic dog or any offers of trifle or lemon meringue pie. But I did check my sandwiches for dog hairs.

On our drive back to London, James said he'd love to see me again and why didn't I bring round some of my famous cooking that he's heard so much about? So on Friday night I'm taking dinner over to his Fulham flat. A private space where we can get to know each other better.

The Baby Belling in my bedsit can barely boil a tin of beans, so I have to cook this meal at school. My Awful Offal lesson gives me a chance to demonstrate chicken liver paté so that's the first course done. At break time I'm cooking Robert Carrier's recipe for Beef Bourguignon. Beef, garlic and tiny onions get thrown into my orange Le Creuset casserole, I tip in a bottle of red wine, then into the oven for three hours. Soon my room smells like a fine Parisian bistro and I just hope Mr Shield won't pop in and ask what's cooking. For dessert, which I'm sure posh James would call pudding, it's profiteroles with chocolate sauce which I'll make at the end of the school day. The way to a man's heart is through his stomach so this feast should lead to some serious seduction.

The traffic's very busy on my drive to Fulham and I arrive late. We unload the dishes from my car and climb the stairs to the kitchen where a pale, straggly girl is propped against the door frame. James lives at a smart address but this flat is a dump and looks like no-one's tidied or cleaned up for years.

'This is Amy, Jenny. She shares the flat and she's been stood up tonight so I said she could join us.'

While James scoots down to get some wine from the off licence, Amy and I set about laying the kitchen table. It's clear she's not pleased with my visit as she thuds down three settings of chipped plates and mismatched cutlery and I hope I can hide my fury that she's sharing my meal.

We start with my pot of paté served with butter curls that outdo his mother's and a basket of crisp Melba toast.

'Help yourselves, please.'

I get a warm feeling that James is impressed as he smiles, mumbles a contented 'Yum' and strokes my arm. Amy prods her paté and refills her wine glass without asking. I think I understand why her date left her. I wouldn't want to take this sulky girl out anywhere and I wish she would clear off to her bedroom and leave us alone to enjoy a romantic dinner.

Now for the beef casserole. James lifts the Le Creuset lid and there's that Ah! Bisto! moment when you inhale wafts of meaty fragrance with the promise of deliciousness to come. So far this meal has been a triumph and I'm pleased to hear another, well deserved 'Yum.'

James clears the table and does not comment as he removes Amy's plate of mashed up, poked about, uneaten food. No wonder she's so thin.

Finally, da da! A stack of golden profiteroles filled with whipped cream and served with a jug of hot, glistening chocolate sauce. This meal couldn't have been more spectacular and now it's surely time for my moment with James. Alone. Amy sticks to her chair. She's not budging and James is not asking her to leave. His flat has no lounge and he's not suggesting we visit his bedroom. I've no chance here tonight. Amy's done for us.

He helps me pack up and load my car with dirty dishes.

'Wonderful meal,' says James. 'I'll give you a call.'

Amy is glowering, or maybe smiling from the top of the stairs.

Trip to the butchers

My trip with my students, out of school, is not going far, just to the butcher's shop at the end of the road to learn about meat. He's showing us how to joint a carcass of lamb and persuading them that cheap cuts can be tasty.

Large posters showing outlines of pig, beef and lamb are pinned on my classroom wall, free from the Meat and Livestock Commission. The animals have cuddly faces but the rest of their bodies look like a chainsaw massacre with hacked up body parts. Students must learn the names of each cut and why the cuts are tough or tender. We can't afford to cook the tender bits like fillet steak, but we can make dishes from cheap cuts of meat, like Lancashire hot pot and many things out of mince.

Students need a reason to leave the school grounds and none should trot out of the school without permission.

My note home for the butcher outing goes like this:

Dear Parent /Guardian

Next week I am taking my Home Economics group to the local butchers to learn about meat.

Please could you give permission for me to take .... out of school for this lesson?

Please sign below

I agree that (Name of student) ....can go on the visit.

Signed Dated

Miss Hyde, Head of Home Economics

The week before the outing is tense. If I don't get all the signed forms back we can't go. I suspect that several signatures are fake, just like the sick notes or the letters explaining why Jimmy couldn't do his homework.

A local newspaper reporter is coming to interview us and take snaps, and I hope it will raise my subject profile and get the school some publicity. I've stressed to him the importance of teaching both boys and girls how to cook in this modern world of sharing home life.

The butcher heaves a lamb carcass onto the thick wooden block and sharpens his knife on his steel. This is manly, grown up stuff. He deftly cuts fleshy chunks of meat from the bones, and reduces the lamb to chops, shoulder and leg. Then finally, the cheapest cut that we will cook in school – the rather fatty but very delicious breast of lamb.

I wait for news of our visit in the local paper. Will we make the front page?

Oh, the disappointment. For all my talk of modern men and women sharing family tasks, the reporter has chosen to put us on page three with the headline -

'It's not easy for mum, is it?'

'Miss Hyde says the idea is that girls should get a visual impression of the cutting up of pork and lamb, in addition to what they learn from their textbooks.'

Oh no I didn't. There's a photo of the girls smiling at the butcher and his dead beast. What about the boys who were there?

It's too late. The reporter has reinforced the stereotype of mum doing the shopping and cooking, and boys and dads taking no part.

One day, I'll get things changed. One day.

Back at school, the butcher delivers a pile of plump lamb breasts with strict instructions that they must be the same size and not cost more than 50 pence each. I don't want an 'It ain't fair' war.

'Gather round and watch carefully. The rib bones must be carefully cut from the flesh of the breast.'

Bert thumps Len and mutters 'Breast.'

'Be quiet. This is important.'

I use my VERY STERN VOICE for this serious task.

We give each of them a tray with a New Zealand Lamb stamped breast and a sharpened filleting knife.

'Boning meat is a very skilled task and I want no fooling around. Do not walk about with these knives.'

We'll count the knives back in at the end of the lesson and no-one will leave the room until all are returned.

Cynthia and I pace the group like lions watching their young at play, encouraging, warning, and keeping an eye on their safety. We collect the bones, fat and gristle in a large bin for Mr Davey in geography to take home for his dog.

'Spread the flattened lamb with sage and onion stuffing, roll it up and tie it like this.'

I show them how to tie the joint with string using a butcher's knot.

There are no more quips. No chat back. Miss is deadly serious and she will take no nonsense.

A line of neatly tied, rolled stuffed breasts of lamb is displayed for marking. The butcher would be proud to sell them in his shop.

'I'll cook these so they are ready to eat at home tonight.'

I don't want anyone munching on raw lamb on the bus.

They pack, hand in their knives and leave. The room fills with smells of roasting lamb and sage and onion stuffing. Nourishing and nurturing smells. These new skills will set them up for family meals in the future – and they might even pass the EXAM.

Vegetarian cooking

Cranks just off Carnaby Street is surely the most fashionable vegetarian restaurant in London. Its mung beans, brown rice and lentil salads were rather too worthy for Mark's and my taste. Our noses took us north to the meaty smells of the Charlotte Street tavernas for kebabs and Retsina. Fond memories of our summer holiday in Corfu. Now spoilt by Sandy.

Today's lesson is about Vegetarians and I get the students to read out passages from textbooks. She Who Ran Away has left me piles of pristine, unopened books to use for the EXAMS.

Asking some boys to read aloud can lead to deep embarrassment as they stumble over words and they don't want others to realise their low reading age. I've chosen clever Linda to begin, but I should have checked the text first. The first textbook has some shocking stuff on vegetarian cooking.

'A vegetarian diet has limited choice and can be monotonous, bulky and unattractive. It is most difficult to supply protein as the protein in beans is of lower biological value so more must be eaten. This may lead to enlargements so the stomach is very full after each meal.'

Oh no. Who wrote this? I want to shout back.

'Monotonous. Unattractive. I'd find a daily bag of chips and a can of cola monotonous.

The pitta bread stuffed with salad and freshly fried falafel eaten from a Marrakech market stall is not unattractive.'

And saying that vegetarian food makes the stomach full after a meal. Surely that's the point? Food should fill us up.

Alice reads on.

'The vegetarian diet may be expensive.'

More silent screaming from me.

How? Compare the cost of baked beans to a rump steak.

They must practice the exam style question for homework as the textbook bible supports the exam.

'Question. What are the difficulties in arranging and preparing meals for vegetarians? How would you overcome these difficulties? Give one day's meals for a vegetarian family of a father, mother and schoolboy son.'

Ahhh!

I open another textbook with its virgin, unturned pages to see if it is more helpful for my vegetarian lesson.

'Meat and fish have distinctive flavours which stimulate the digestive juices and increase the appetite. In a vegetarian diet these flavours are sadly missing.'

Noooo! Isn't that the point? A vegetarian doesn't eat animals so they would hate these 'distinctive meaty, fishy flavours.'

'Larger portions of vegetables should be served to vegetarians than to those eating a normal diet.'

So vegetarians aren't normal? They don't eat a normal diet and must eat platefuls of vegetables.

How am I going to teach this nonsense?
At the end there are some exam style questions:

Question 1. Why are meatless dishes often unpopular? How can this be avoided?

Question 2. What are the difficulties in arranging and preparing meals for a vegetarian?

Imagine how my classes will answer.

Question 1 Answer:

Meatless dishes are unpopular 'cos they don't have any meat in them. This can be avoided by not eating them.

Question 2 Answer:

The difficulties in arranging and preparing meals for a vegetarian are that they need lots of beans and vegetables to get their protein and this can be expensive. They get full and enlarged.

Help. Throw these books in the bin and realise there are millions of vegetarians around the world. Rewrite the books. How many more students in our multicultural society will have to put up with this nonsense? Blah!

Nut cutlets are today's vegetarian recipe demonstration, made from chopped nuts and breadcrumbs, shaped into cutlets and then fried. If vegetarians don't eat meat, why the hell do they make their recipes look like the body parts of a lamb? The fried, nutty bits are so horrid that even Bert, my food dustbin, refuses to taste. My battered *Vegetarianism for Beginners* advertises Nutter 'The Ideal Vegetable Cooking Fat.' That name's as daft as guessing what my subject is called. I think the manufacturers need to call a board meeting and call it something like Pelican or Crow to compete with Stork margarine.

Dawn, the school secretary, pops in after the end of school bell.

'Glad I caught you, Jenny. Mr Shield wants to talk to you about Cynthia's hours. And a man called James says can you phone him when you've finished work this afternoon. He'll wait in his office for your call.'

She hands me a folded paper with a city telephone number. Well, well. She closes my door with a glance of disapproval.

The Gas Board cometh

The Gas and Electricity Boards have kindly installed cookers on free hire for my room and there must be equal numbers for each fuel so my students can compare their cooking experiences. But more likely I think I am in the unwitting vanguard for an energy supply war. Every two years the cookers are replaced with newer models, so I've got my eye on the Cordon Bleu with its huge double oven and eye level grill when it gets discarded. The next occupant of my bedsit can keep the mean spirited Baby Belling as I'll move into a new spacious home to cook elaborate dinner parties for all my friends. Well, a girl can dream.

The weirdest appliance in my food room is the gas-fired refrigerator which clunks away behind my desk. Yes. A noisy, cumbersome box on free loan from the Gas Board to make sure I treat each of the power suppliers the same. The pilot light at the top has an annoying habit of blowing out and needs relighting before the melting ice cubes puddle onto the floor. The most stupid thing is that the gas-fired fridge has to be plugged into electricity to run the light that comes on when the door is opened so this fuel competition is pointless.

In Gas and Electricity showrooms around the country, shiny new ranges of cookers are on display and helpful home economists guide shoppers in their cooker choice. And joy upon joy, they are willing to send these lovely ladies into school for cookery demonstrations.

Today Sue and Sandra from the local Gas showroom are visiting to cook a three course meal in the GAS oven to show us how to save fuel and to use the new automatic timers. No doubt the exam boards will invent more daft questions.

'Describe how a housewife can use the automatic oven timer to help prepare a meal for her family when they return from a Sunday walk.'

I imagine the answers.

'She can heat up Fray Bentos steak and kidney pies for each of her kids and cook some baked beans in a tin. And me family don't do walks on a Sunday. We go to the pub.'

My O level group is chosen for the Gas Board visit. They'll be respectful to these ladies, and I've briefed them with enthusiastic, intelligent questions. I hope that Carol and Vicky, who have been dumped in this group, have bunked off for the afternoon.

Sue and Sandra arrive early, laden with boxes and baskets for their demonstration. They glance around my room with a look of surprise and I feel its shabbiness. Yes, the open concrete drain running inside the room is a health hazard, the chipped

Formica tops of the cooking units with their battered doors need replacing, and the butlers' sinks would be better used for garden planting. But I've brightened the walls with posters of cows, pigs and lambs showing their body parts, and the colourful map of English cheeses.

'Ladies, mind your heads on those cables dangling from the ceiling. We plug the irons into them for our shirt ironing lesson, but if you're tall like me, they can bang you on the head.'

Sue and Sandra duck through the maze of black, hanging wires and set up their demonstration beside the new Cordon Bleu cooker, shining from my early morning clean.

The class has lined up quietly outside and now they are invited onto their stools. Shhh. No talking.

I introduce Sue and Sandra.

'These ladies are your local Gas Board Home Service Advisors and your family can visit them when you buy a new cooker.'

No mention of the Electricity Showroom nearby.

'Hello to you all. Very pleased to meet you.'

Sue is confident and clear – she'd make a good teacher.

'We're going to show you this new cooker and how to use the automatic timer. So useful if your mother wants to have a meal ready when you all return home from an outing.'

She hands round the Gas Board menu for our special three course meal and I'm not asking my class if any fathers cook at home although I know they do.

Starter – Grilled grapefruit topped with brown sugar
Main course – Roasted lamb chops with potato wedges and frozen peas
Sweet course – Baked treacle sponge with sauce

'First, let's prepare the grapefruit.'

We watch as they cut zig zags around the middle of the grapefruit, then split it into two perfect halves.

'Sprinkle on some brown sugar, and could three of you prepare the rest, so there's enough for you all to taste.'

Oven cooked, sugar topped grapefruit – what a treat. I hope the group will remember this dish for their practical exam.

'Next, scrunch some foil round the top of the lamb chops to stop them burning, put them on a roasting tray with the potato quarters and dot with knobs of lard. The frozen peas go in this foil pouch with a knob of butter.'

Butter. Butter. We can't afford butter. Thank goodness the boys aren't here. They'd ask how big the knobs are and I'd be embarrassed.

Bang. Bang. Carol and Vicky burst in.

'Are we cooking Miss?'

'Sit on your stools girls. We're really lucky to have this demonstration and there'll be something for you to taste later.'

They thump down, quietened by the seriousness of the rest of the class.

'Now girls. Make the sponge by the all-in-one method – put all the ingredients in a bowl and beat with electric beaters.'

My group doesn't let on that they know this already. It's pudding for tasting after all.

'Spoon the golden syrup into the cake tin and smooth the sponge evenly over the top. Heat up some golden syrup with water for the sauce when you are ready to serve.'

Why is treacle sponge made with golden syrup? Don't ask. Carol and Vicky, please don't ask.

'Put all of these dishes in the oven at once, set the timer so it comes on by itself. At home your mother can set the timer so that the meal is ready when your family all comes in together. Like after Sunday church or …'

They see me wince. Please don't describe any more Gas Board happy family situations. You might find out what it's really like at home.

'Girls, let's cook this now so you can have a taste.'

While the lamb chops sizzle, Sue and Sandra demonstrate the wonders of the Cordon Bleu cooker with its smart rotisserie and tools and spikes that we will never use. We can't afford CHICKEN or anything else to spike and rotate.

I've chalked up a time-filling question on the black roller board.

'Class. This is a question you might get in the EXAM, so answer it while Sue and Sandra pack away.'

I read aloud.

'Describe the special features of a gas cooker that you consider important. Write out a menu for a three course dinner and say how you would use the cooker to prepare this meal for a family of four.'

'Answer the question, please. Carol and Vicky, can you lay the table ready for our tasting?'

The pair know where my tablecloths and cutlery are kept and would rather fuss and lay the table than do any written work.

The three course meal is ready. They crowd round and eat hot bits of baked grapefruit, lamb chops, roast potato chunks, peas and spoonfuls of treacle sponge.

'Let's say thankyou to the Gas Board ladies for a splendid demonstration.'

We clap as these two hard working women pack up their boxes and bags and head wearily back to the showroom. What a brilliant afternoon, and I've had a rest from teaching.

As they leave I hand out another exam board question for practice.

'Question. Show how to prepare a) a gas oven, b) an electric oven for baking a cake. Give information on the regular cleaning of a gas or electric oven.'

Thanks to Sue and Sandra they can answer the gas oven bit but the electric cookers were never mentioned. I'll need to get the Electricity Board home economists in to balance things up.

The cane

A row of boys is slouched outside the headmaster's study, some leaning against the wall, others squatting on the floor. Several are due in my next class but they are not giving me eye contact.

'Tom – what's happening?'

He shrugs and turns away.

'Are you coming to the lesson?'

'Dunno, Miss.'

Tom appears occasionally but I suspect he's got a job elsewhere. He's one of the gang who's not taking any exams so his time at school must seem pointless.

A lad opens the office door and seems downcast until he turns the corner and punches the air with his fist. And I get it. These boys are waiting to be caned. Yuk. The rattan stick, which I assume is a cane, was propped on the wall behind Mr Shield's desk on my last visit to ask for more funds, but whatever goes on in his room is the stuff of legend. There's so much I want to know.

Do girls and boys both get beaten?

Do they have to bend over the desk like Billy Bunter in the BBC comedy about Greyfriars School?

Does he give them six of the best or is it just one whack?

Is it bottom or hand?

Mr Shield has an unlikely stature and presence for a headmaster. He's a small, inoffensive man and he sometimes stands outside my window, puts his thumbs in his ears and wiggles his fingers. I'm surprised he doesn't stick his tongue out like young children do in the playground.

Gavin is often threatened with caning for general school disruption but staffroom gossip says that Mr Shield is not fast enough to clobber him.

One evening, a friend's father tells me, in a very firm voice, that corporal punishment is essential to keep order in the classroom and he hopes I use my rolling pins to give them a bash.

'I was caned every day at school, Jenny, and it never did me any harm. Can you hit them?'

How I long to reply: 'If you had to be caned every day it can't have done you much good.'

I've never sent anyone to be caned. Students who come in after a caning session seem chastened. Their resentment lingers and they are not ready to take part in lessons.

My own discipline methods don't always go to plan.

One day when Andrew was drumming on a saucepan with a wooden spoon, I suggested that he calmed down and took a long walk round the lake. And come back when he'd cooled down.

The class busied themselves making Cornish pasties when I noticed that he'd gone.

'Where's Andrew?'

Tom offered some help.

'You told him to go round the lake, Miss.'

Oh Gawd – the Remedial department has sent Andrew to my lessons and told me to give him clear instructions when he's cooking. Seems like he's followed my round the lake one literally. What if he's cooled off by jumping in? We're not supposed to tell students to walk out of our classes and leave school. Or go and jump in lakes.

I worry through the lesson but am pleased when as the bell rings, Andrew returns to collect his kit bag.

A rolled up newspaper with a targeted tap on the shoulder is my simple method to get attention. That stopped when one day someone put a rolling pin inside – I thought it seemed heavier.

Occasionally, very occasionally, I implement my Vulcan Grip. This undetectable technique involves pressing my thumb firmly between the muscles of the upper arm of a badly behaved boy who is usually bigger than me.

'Your behaviour is unreasonable and dangerous. Please stop it.'

All the time I quietly give instructions. The arm squeeze looks gentle and it hurts, but the large boy has never protested. So far it successfully ends the trouble and keeps a busy class cooking safely.

It's nearly the end of the term for my French evening class and we're meeting for supper in a local restaurant. The group has become really friendly and all this term I've looked forward to our Monday classes and the pub meetup afterwards. One weekend a few of us met for a stroll round Hampstead Heath then a delicious tea and cakes at Louis Patisserie in the village. I love the old world Hungarian feel of this tearoom, the crispiest Mille Feuille and my hot tea served in a glass cup with a slice of lemon on a saucer with a frilly d'oyley. That's style.

Our restaurant tonight is buzzing with customers and they've reserved a large table for our group. The menu is beautifully bistro and it's easy to make a quick choice of French onion soup, Coquille St Jacques and Crème Caramel from the menu. Daniel sits next to me and I wonder if the group will think something is going on between us. I'd be embarrassed if they did. His wedding ring looks very gold tonight. That musky smell of patchouli wafts whenever he leans over to pour me a glass of wine. It's very distracting.

The meal is a jolly affair. We josh with the waiters with our 'Mercis' and 'au revoirs' but I'm not sure they understand our food ordering in evening class French.

Before we leave, Daniel puts an idea to the group.

'You know, in the summer term, we should all have a weekend together in Paris. We get on so well.'

'Just the group or should partners come along too?' asks one of the married women.

'No, just this class. We could practise our French with the locals.'

Daniel will be away from his wife. Now that's something to look forward to.

Invalid cooking

Why, oh why do I have to teach Invalid Cooking? It ranks lower than Awful Offal in educational pointlessness. We're supposed to make our lessons real and relevant to teenage needs, but I'm teaching the skills of Mrs Beeton. And she died at twenty eight so clearly her staff were not successful with serving her invalid food.

This is an exam task that we have to practice:

'Plan a meal for an invalid. Lay the tray with a starched tray cloth and serve the meal.'

We need to cook for a sick person AND starch and iron a tray cloth to put on an invalid tray. Mrs Beeton, eat your heart out. This exam needs changing.

When I was ill as a child my mother cycled off to her teaching job and left me a bowl of banana custard for lunch. My grandmother would pop in and check if I was OK, but otherwise I was left alone with no telly for comfort. When I was really ill when I had tonsillitis, the banana custard had a glacé cherry on top. I reckon my mother would have been charged with child neglect if that happened today. Since I started teaching, I've never taken sick leave. And now I'm sad as I don't imagine anyone would bring me a tray of invalid food if I was sick, alone in my bedsit.

So what shall we cook for today's invalid lesson?

Our textbook bible has some dreadful choices – junket, egg jelly, savoury custard, baked fish, cheese pudding, apple snow and fruit fools.

'Class – we need a meal for an invalid. Something that they don't have to chew.'

'Don't invalids have teeth, Miss?' Carol is pretending to be serious. Perhaps she could train as a nurse or social worker if she gets her exams. This lesson may have some point after all. And where is Vicky?

'Me Nan never puts her teeth in when she eats. Only when

she goes to Bingo. She takes her curlers out and puts her teeth in.'

Bert is trying to raise our spirits. I imagine his Nan reminding herself before she goes out.

'Teeth in, curlers out, get Bingo money.'

I hold up a black and white photo of steamed cod in white sauce with cauliflower from the Good Housekeeping recipe book.

'Invalids need to eat nourishing food that is easy to eat like this.'

'Looks like sick, Miss – who would eat that when you're sick?'

'I had baked beans, mashed potato and ice cream when I had me tonsils out.'

'Carol and Bert, we've got to do it – it's in the EXAM. Now I'm making junket.'

This is going back a hundred years. I've never seen or eaten junket. Ever.

'Watch while I demonstrate.'

They like sitting on stools with the chance to tut and test my patience.

'Warm the milk to body temperature then add the rennet. That's from the enzyme, rennin, that comes from a calf's stomach. It clots the milk and makes it set.'

I pour the junket into a glass sundae dish and pop it in the fridge to set.

'Miss, we ain't tasting that.'

It's Carol and I secretly agree. Why should they taste something that's made from an ingredient from a calf's stomach that's mixed into milk just to make junket for some sick person? Their mad cooking teacher has landed from Planet Pointless again, demanding that they use suffering animals to make inedible food that will be tipped down the sink when they get out of this crazy lesson.

Let's get this over with.

'Watch while I demonstrate cod with cauliflower.'

White cauliflower florets get tipped into boiling water, a tiny piece of cod on an enamel plate goes on top, then cover and cook. Terry makes the all-in-one white sauce and the room smells of boiled fish and cauliflower, just like the school kitchens at nine in the morning.

I read out the Rules for Laying a Tray for Invalids, as Terry cooks on.

'When the doctor orders the invalid to have a light diet, the meals must be served punctually, as they are the main interest of the day. If the invalid does not want to eat at the appointed time, remove the meal and re-serve it later.'

The invalid tray is the next task which will finally prove that I have landed from Doctor Who's Time Machine, from an age long ago when we lived on turnips.

'Make sure the patient has all the accompaniments – salt, pepper, butter – and add flowers in tiny posies in small low vases which cannot be knocked over and a table napkin.'

Great. Bob, the school gardener, will love me as his borders are raided for roses and posies to plonk on the bloody tray.

The CSE exam has one more horror. We have to wash and starch a tray cloth using powdered starch, made into a paste with boiling water. Once again, I am teaching home crafts from a museum age.

Please let this lesson end.

'We need a tray cloth and napkin, matching china and cutlery, cruets, butter dishes and a small posy. Use a tray of suitable size and arrange all serving dishes so that they are easy for use.'

So that's a tray the size of a small table. Gawd almighty.

I place the steamed cod and cauliflower, junket and a glass of water on the tray and IT'S DONE.

We've DONE invalid cooking.

There are two questions for homework from their textbook.

1. State six points that should be kept in mind in the choice, preparation and serving of foods for invalids. Give reasons.

2. What differences in diet would you suggest for a) a bed-ridden elderly person, b) a convalescent from pneumonia?

I'll look forward to the answers and hope someone makes me laugh.

'Would anyone like to eat my cod and cauliflower?'

Terry sums up for the rest of the class.

'Na thanks Miss, no-one here is sick.'

Easter is coming

It's nearly the Easter holidays and I'm happy and sad that so many are leaving school. They've turned sixteen and can finish with school for good. I'm happy for them as they are fed up attending meaningless lessons when they are not taking any exams. And happy that they are looking forward to their grown up life outside school.

Sad, as I'll miss their cheek and humour. Sad, because I wonder how they will manage without any qualifications – not even basic exams in Maths and English. Sad, because some of them will not get the chance to show the potential that I believe they have.

Some like Len and Carol have popped by to say goodbye. Vicky has not been in school for days and I worry for her. Alan dithers around the school corridors and I doubt if I'll see him before the term ends, if indeed he remembers the end of term date. And I wonder if John will find a job in a garage where he can test drive some cars instead of stealing them. There's no news of Gavin, which must please most of us who have had the misfortune of having him blunder in and disrupt our lessons. I think we'll read about him in the local newspapers now he's reached reporting age.

Before I close up my room for Easter and hope Jim and the cleaners will give it a good scrub, I check my desk drawer before it's locked. A tiny Cadbury's Creme Egg is inside, wrapped in red, purple and gold foil with a small bit of paper torn from a notebook. 'Thanks Miss Len.' As I bite through the chocolate shell into the white and yellow filling I remember how carefully I made them crack my eggs to separate the yolks from the whites. I hope Len is going to be alright.

Over the Easter break I'll drive down to the Sussex coast where my parents have a holiday flat overlooking the sea. We'll spend days filled with sunshine, cycling along the coastal path and walking the wide sandy beaches. Wild sea spinach and purple sea kale grow in the dunes and we'll pick the young spring leaves and cook them in a little butter. No margarine for my parents. It's amazing how the leaves retain the taste of the salt and the sea. Bob, the young fisherman who has a shed below the flats, brings in his daily catch with a choice of crab, skate or some plaice flapping about if it's just landed.

Now I've decided to stay in my job, I'm going to see if I can buy a small house in a cheaper area of London like Finsbury Park. There are rows of small terraced houses that need doing up and I need something to look forward to. Perhaps on a visit to The Loose Box I'll find a B for Builder to help. This single life is taking its toll.

Summer Term 1973

Using leftovers

Jim and his team have worked hard during the holidays and made the school smell clean and shiny. I always feel a whiff of excitement at the start of a new term. Clean beginnings, refreshed and ready to learn after our break. I'm happy to be back.

The deputy head has left a note on my desk.

'Carol has decided not to leave at Easter and will return to your classes to take her exams.'

No. Please no. Carol with no exercise book, no pen and who's already lost one textbook that I can't afford to replace. Carol can cook a Governor's tea and a few jam tarts but never brings her ingredients. Carol who storms out if I catch her doing something I don't like. Carol who says my lessons are rubbish. Who on earth persuaded Carol to stay on?

Now I am supposed to get Carol exam-ready in a few weeks. How can I teach her to cook a two course meal and some cakes and pastries? And pass a written exam? How?

Onwards and upwards, they are ready for my lesson on Rechauffé cooking or in plain English, Learning about Leftovers. My mother is an expert in using leftover food. Sunday's leftover roast meat becomes cottage pie or rissoles, leftover Brussels sprouts and potatoes are fried into bubble and squeak and stale bread is made into bread and butter pudding or breadcrumbs. She once showed me her ration book from the war and I reckon the food shortages are the reason why she makes us eat everything on our plates before we can leave the table.

The problem with my Rechauffé lesson is that we haven't got any leftovers. I've been away over the holidays and there's not a scrap of food in my bedsit, and no-one wants to bring in their leftover scraps to show the rest of the class. It's like holding up your holey socks from the darning basket.

They're on their usual stools around my demonstration table. Carol for once seems quiet.

I read from our textbook.

'An extravagant cook will throw extra cooked food away.

An unimaginative one simply warms it up or serves it cold.

An efficient one will deal with it in such a way as to present an attractive, appetising and nutritious dish.'

Their aprons are on ready, waiting while I read out THE RULES.

'Class, Learn this for the EXAM. Rule 1. Leftover food must be absolutely fresh.'

'Yes, Alice?'

Please, don't ask the obvious question.

'How can leftover food be fresh, Miss?'

'Good point, Alice – it means it mustn't be stale.'

'But, Miss you said to use stale bread – you said...'

'Rule 2. Reheat the food only – do not re-cook.'

Stupid, stupid books – how do you reheat without cooking?

'Listen – we must not waste food. Think about how your grandparents managed during the war. The posters said 'Make do and Mend' and food was scarce.'

'Me grandfather ate army food during the war – he was a soldier.'

Tim wants to cook and is fed up with talking.

'OK. Next Rule. When you reheat leftover food it must be piping hot to kill the germs.'

'How do you know when it's piping hot?'

Good question Alice. Stick your finger in it and shout 'Ow, it's piping hot.'

I don't know – perhaps you test it with a pipe.

'We're making fishcakes today with leftover potatoes, bread and tinned salmon.'

Cynthia has boiled a large saucepan full of potatoes for our leftovers and she's baked slices of an old Mother's Pride loaf in the oven until they are crisp, so that's more leftovers. They've each got a tin of pink salmon. Except for Carol.

'Class. This is how you make the breadcrumbs.'

I seal the crunchy bread slices inside a polythene bag, bash it loudly with a rolling pin and hold up the crumbs for them to admire.

'But they're brown. Breadcrumbs are orange.'

No wonder Tim is jumpy if he's eating orange coloured Paxo packet breadcrumbs.

'Now it's your turn, class.'

They scatter and mash the potato with the pink fish, season then shape the mash into fishcakes. Carol is making plain potato cakes.

'Dip in beaten egg and then roll in breadcrumbs and they're ready to cook.'

A dipping and rolling queue lines up at my table. A pushy line with the occasional thump. We melt our knob of lard in frying pans and cook our fishcakes until they are crisp and golden.

'Marking please.'

Plates of crunchy fishcakes served on a plain d'oyley and decorated with a sprig of parsley appear on my table. Sit down. We're ready to eat. Hot and delicious with some salad cream.

For homework they must learn some réchauffé recipes. Cooked meat makes Durham cutlets, meat in aspic, kromeskies and mince toast. Where did these peculiar dishes come from? Thank goodness Réchauffé and Invalid cooking are done and dusted for another year.

My French evening classes have started up again and the group is happy to be together. There's a freshness in the spring evenings and it'll soon be warm enough to take our drinks out into the pub garden. Daniel hangs back as we leave. Can we meet one evening this week for a drink?

Drinka Pinta Milka Day

In the 1960s every school child was allowed a third of a pint of free milk at morning break time. At the Girls' High School that I attended, my sixth form prefect job was the milk monitor – more of a punishment than a badge of honour. Every day I stuck paper straws through the silver foil caps of tiny, glass milk bottles, and handed them out to girls that chose to come along. Empty bottles were collected and washed out to be stacked on top of the ever increasing crates of unopened ones to be returned to the milkman. In cold winter months, if the crates were left outside, blue tits pecked holes in the foil to get at the cream. My other much hated role was to strip off the broken caps before girls spotted this unhygienic damage.

It is no surprise that milk has lost its popularity among teenagers.

In 1971 Margaret Thatcher ended free school milk and got loud chants of 'Maggie Thatcher, Milk Snatcher.' Many are relieved to see the end of break time milk, which led to crates of wasted bottles. Others complain that the nation's children will suffer nutritional deficiencies. The move saves the government twenty million pounds in times of financial cutbacks.

At school I have stacks of National Dairy Council booklets encouraging us to drink and cook with milk, and free posters to decorate my classroom showing *How the Cow makes Milk*, and *Milk Nutrition*. TV adverts from The Milk Marketing Board persuade us to Drinka Pinta Milka Day, and local milkmen deliver pints of milk in glass bottles to most doorsteps in the country. The government wants us to drink more milk and it seems to be my job to support this mission. It's Milk, Milk, Milk everywhere.

'Class, today we're going to taste some different types of milk.'

I've chosen bottles with a range of coloured foil tops and chilled them in the gas refrigerator.

They must learn to identify the milk tops by the colour – for the EXAM. It's a popular and easy question.

Gold for rich and creamy Channel Island milk, silver for whole milk, red for homogenised and red and silver for the new semi-skimmed.

Sterilised milk comes in tall, thin stemmed glass bottles with red writing on the glass and has a fluted metal cap that I flip off with a beer bottle opener. Sterilised milk keeps for ages and is popular in homes without a fridge. I wonder if it's a leftover wartime taste.

'Me granddad always has this milk with his tea. Won't drink nothin else.' It's perky Bert, fresh from his Easter break.

Cynthia pours each milk into separate jugs so they can't identify the contents by the foil top.

We start with the gold foil top – Jersey and Guernsey. Creamy, golden, sumptuous. As a child I longed for the top two inches of thick yellow cream to pour out first onto my cornflakes.

Silver top is our pale, bland, everyday milk, with a thin cream line.

Homogenised, the red foil top, is the modern choice, mixed and heated to make every pour the same, and no cream line.

Semi skimmed seems thin and weedy, and Sterilised milk tastes boiled and sweet.

They pour, sip and taste, vote and tally the marks so we get the most popular choice.

Surprise, surprise. It's the silver top. The one they drink at home. The one they had for free at infants' school. Sterilised milk comes a close second. Perhaps a taste from their grandparents.

Now for their treat. Cynthia whizzes the remaining milks with ice, red jam, and chocolate powder in the huge jug on top of the Kenwood mixer to make each of them a chocolate and raspberry milkshake, then pours it into glasses. No one cares what milk it is made from as long as they get a coloured straw.

Tonight I'm meeting Daniel at a pub near Primrose Hill – but not the one where the French group drink. Just in case. He's already sitting at the bar when I arrive, his pint of beer resting on a pile of paper. 'You know the idea of the French group going to Paris? Well, I've been finding out more. We can get a short flight from Lydd Airport to Le Touquet and then a bus to Paris and we could stay in a hotel that I know near Notre-Dame. Leave on Friday night back Sunday evening. What do you think?'

'Won't you need to check with the rest of the group? See if they agree?'

'I thought it could be just the two of us.' Wow. I'm stunned. What about the wife? What about Mark? Where the hell is Lydd airport? I've only flown from Gatwick and Heathrow.

'Tell people that ask that we're all going to Paris with our French class. To practise. Only the group will be just the two of us. We're too late for the cherry blossom but how will a weekend in May suit you?'

He moves to get up. It's that patchouli perfume again. Dark woods, damp moss and the smell of the earth. A weekend with Daniel in May will suit me very well.

'Can I have your address and your car registration in case I need to contact you?'

I pencil the street and house number round the edge of his beer mat but I can't remember my car number plate. Ever.

'It's a green Mini Traveller – wood timbered, moss growing on the window ledges, ancient, usually parked outside my bedsit house and never cleaned. It should be easy to spot.'

'Daniel – out of interest – what do you do?'

'Chartered Surveyor.' Now that fits into my Loose Box A-C list of jobs on my manhunt.

It's a warm spring evening and I wish we could go back to my room – well not that room, a less miserable room. The cherry tree outside my window is in blossom and it flowers in two colours – white and vivid pink. Something to do with grafting a white branch onto a pink one and it's light enough to show him. But my housemates might tell the landlord of my nighttime visitor and I'd be booted out. We'll have to wait until Paris.

How mucky is it?

Bert comes in and pinches the top of my arm.

'Pinch, punch, first of the month Miss.' Rude boy.

Their theory paper in June is really worrying me. We've got less than two months before the exam and they go on study leave after May half term. That's just a month to drill in some knowledge.

Today is my food hygiene and safety lesson and I'm doing experiments to show them the hazards in the cookery room. I think they remember stuff better if I show them rather than read it in books. Michael, the science technician, has lent me some Petri dishes from his chemistry cupboard and I've filled them with agar jelly which I've made from strands of agar, bought from London's Chinatown. It's the perfect medium for growing bacteria and mould.

The class sits round my demonstration table watching a row of plastic dishes filled with gelatinous jelly.

'This jelly is made from agar, which is a seaweed and we're going to use it to grow some germs. Where do you think we will find the most germs in this room?'

They stare back. Their eyes have a fierce, quiet message.

'We want to cook not do this stupid science stuff.'

I scratch BACTERIA AND MOULD with chalk on the black roller board.

'Let's start with unwashed hands. Carol – press your fingers onto this jelly.'

A low moan comes from Bert.

'Listen – the quicker we do this experiment, the sooner you can cook.'

The class glares at Bert to shut up.

'Now I'll put a lid on the dish, seal it with tape and label it Fingers.'

'What else might be dirty in this room?'

Stupid, stupid question. I scowl at the boys and hope I didn't hear 'knickers'.

'What about dishcloths? Someone fetch me one.'

Terry presses a soggy dishcloth firmly into the jelly leaving a knitted imprint. Lid on, sealed, taped, labelled Dishcloth.

'Another dirty thing please.'

'Hair.' Ouch. Some strands of hair get pulled out, stuck to the jelly and labelled Hair.

'Linda – suggest something else we can test for bacteria.'

'Spit, Miss.'

Sensible, sensible Linda is another girl who comes to this class under sufferance. She was too meek to ask to change to Technical Drawing, and gets on with her cooking quietly out of the boys' radar.

'Good idea – who'd like to spit into the Petri dish?'

Ray's hand shoots up.

'OK, Ray – take this dish over to the sink and spit into it.'

Ray aims a glob that lands expertly in the middle of the jelly.

Sealed, taped and labelled Spit, it joins the windowsill line up of Fingers, Dishcloth, Hair behind my desk. Along with a Do Not Touch sign.

'This experiment will show you the importance of handwashing before cooking and why I wash all the dishcloths in the twin tub each night and why long hair is tied back. And that's why catering kitchens have notices up saying 'Don't Spit!''

'Just to finish I want to show you how mould grows on food.'

Groan, moan.

I seal some slices of damp Mother's Pride bread in a large

polythene bag. Another bag contains my lunchtime apple core, then both bags join the row of Petri dishes on the windowsill and the Do Not Touch sign.

There are mumblings of 'Miss. Please, let's cook.' So it's aprons on, hair back, hands washed and we're making Cornish pasties, while the Petri dishes work on my hygiene message.

Each morning when I arrive at school I look through the lids to see any changes. It's like keeping a pet goldfish. Each day I am rewarded with expanding rings of colour as the bacteria and mould feed and grow. There are grey, furry splodges of fungal spores on the agar and yellow and orange circles of expanding colonies of bacteria increasing each day. The bread and rotting apple core are growing expansive blue fronds of mould.

We stand round the sealed Petri dishes, each showing multicoloured circles of coloured growths.

'Look class. See how hands, dishcloths, hair and spit all contain bacteria – those coloured rings – and that grey stuff, mould. And that's why we clean up to cook.'

I hold up the two mouldy, smelly bags of bread and apple core which no longer resemble the original contents.

'Miss – we know. We don't eat mouldy stuff.'

'Actually Ray, some moulds are good. Like Blue Stilton cheese.'

They hate blue cheese. They only eat Cheddar.

At the end of school I scrape the contents of the Petri dishes into a bin bag, wash out the dishes and return them to Michael with a lemon curd tart on a d'oyley on a plate.

'Thanks, Michael – we had some really interesting things growing on them.'

'Where are the contents, Jenny?'

'In the bin in my room.'

'What? You know that's SO DANGEROUS. Growing bacterial cultures in your classroom, throwing them in the bin and then washing the dishes. Haven't you heard of the Black Death and

Plague? Bring me your bin bag to dispose of safely and I'll need to autoclave these Petri dishes.'

Oh whoops. I wonder if he'll eat my tart.

Tonight I'm meeting Mark at his flat – well it was our happy flat once upon a time before Sandy. I wonder if she's been back from America to visit. We climb up four flights of stairs then open the flat door which leads up a tiny, steep staircase high into the rooms under the roof space. I gaze out of the lounge windows over the tops of trees just coming into leaf and far over the landscape of west London. How I remember happy parties in this room crowded with friends who brought food and wine and danced till late in the night. It's very tidy and rather cosy but feels quietly unvisited. I need Mark's advice on a house I've seen in north London – a rather dismal area and the property needs complete refurbishment. Mark is good with money and he can explain how to choose a mortgage.

Breakfast

My message for today is chalked on my rollerboard.

'Breakfast is the most important meal of the day. It helps you break your fast, gives you energy to learn things and we all need a really good breakfast to start the day and help us concentrate.'

My own school breakfast is usually a cup of tea sipped through the cigarette haze of the staffroom followed by a Polo mint to give that fresh minty breath before I start teaching. The newsagent near the school has no doubt had a busy breakfast rush hour selling Mars Bars, bags of crisps and fizzy pop. Today, Mr Shield the headmaster has droned on through a particularly long and boring assembly – bla, bla bla – and finished with his usual praise for the school football team, whose kit I no longer have to wash, thank God. So we're late and need to get on.

I wonder how I'm going to inspire the boys who are slumped, dozing on my cooking tables.

'For breakfast make sure you have some breakfast cereal, vitamin C from orange juice or grapefruit, and protein from boiled eggs or bacon, and some toast and a hot drink.'

Bert stuffs some chocolate in his mouth and pushes the crumpled Bounty Bar wrapper into his equipment drawer. The blue and white label with its desert island palm trees reminds me of a lost opportunity when I turned down that chance for a job in Jamaica. An island of sunshine makes London life seem dreary.

'Today we're going to prepare and serve a proper breakfast and lay the table – you might have to make it FOR THE EXAM, so we need to practice.'

This dreaded EXAM is a threat for us all. I have to teach them how to cook a three course breakfast, lay the table properly and pretend this meal is served in households throughout the country.

Our breakfast menu today is:

Half of fresh grapefruit with a glacé cherry. The Citrus Fruit Board is persuading us to eat grapefruit all day.

Fried egg and bacon, grilled tomatoes, fried bread. A small pile Danish Bacon leaflets sit on my desk.

Toast and marmalade and a pot of tea.

I would say toast and butter, but we can only afford margarine.

We shift out toast racks, tea services, cruet sets, mustard pots, marmalade and sugar bowls, cutlery and crockery from the storeroom and lay the tables with seersucker tablecloths and napkins. There's enough crockery and dining equipment in my storeroom to serve breakfast on the Titanic. Our books tell us that seersucker tablecloths are OK for breakfast, but we should use embroidered or lace cloths for afternoon tea. I'll need to explain that to Mr Shield when it comes to increasing my capitation. Again.

'Bring your stools – I'll show you how to prepare the grapefruit. Cut it in half, then use the GRAPEFRUIT KNIFE to cut round and loosen the segments.'

Ah ha – another tool from the food museum. I have a box of these specialist knives, with curved blades and a serrated edge on each side. And they only do one job – cutting grapefruit segments.

My elaborate preparation goes on.

'Snip the edges of the rind with scissors so that it's pointy all the way round. Serve in a glass sundae dish with a glacé cherry on top, on a saucer with a frilly d'oyley and a grapefruit spoon.'

Why do I teach this nonsense? It's a plot from the d'oyley factory to increase production.

The boys are experts at a breakfast fry up. They snip off the bacon rind, melt some lard in the frying pan, fry the bacon and eggs, fry the bread until golden and crispy and grill the tomatoes.

Quick – cook the toast and put it in the toast rack. Don't bother with butter curls. Make pots of steaming tea. Dump the washing up in the butlers' sinks.

'Sit down class, let's eat.'

Passers-by watch through my steamy classroom windows and Mr Lewes teases in the staffroom.

'It's all right for you Jenny. All you do is cook and eat. We slave away at the blackboard trying to impart knowledge then correct piles of exercise books while you just taste their food and give them a mark.'

Yes, right. And who do I see driving off home as soon as the school bell rings? Who sits and listens to the cricket scores on his radio in his hidey hole at the back of his classroom during break time?

But he's got a point – what lesson could be better and more useful than cooking?

Weekend in Paris

It's Friday afternoon and my weekend bag has been packed for ages with new lacy underwear and a slip of a nightdress. I'm ready to fly. Daniel's right about the journey. Our plane to Paris lands in the tiny airport of Le Touquet, but it's bloody miles to Paris and I'm grumpy that hours of our precious, short time together are spent bumping along with other thrifty weekenders on an old bus along old French roads with potholes. But he's done well with our hotel, a stone's throw from Notre-Dame and the nearby Seine. A grand *fin du siècle* place.The elderly concierge grasps the ornate wrought iron banisters to steady herself as she leads the way up the stone staircase. Up, up and up to the fourth floor. Double doors unlock into an enormous room, with a huge bed stacked with soft pillows and what feels like linen sheets. She points proudly into the bathroom at the massive enamel bath standing high up on its lion's claw feet. An antique, big enough for two. I wonder if Daniel has booked the honeymoon suite.

'Voila. Madame, Monsieur. Bienvenue.'

Daniel hands her a tip and she's gone. How clever to register us as Mr and Mrs Smith and thank goodness she didn't ask for our passports. He opens the long glass windows onto the balcony and we stand together looking down, down onto the bustling Paris street. It's the first time we've been inside any room alone on our own. The giant bath takes ages to fill with warm foamy suds and there's plenty of room for two as we face each other, playing footsie and rejoicing in our luck. For now, the bright lights from the bars and restaurants will have to wait. Smells of cooking drift upwards. People are chattering and eating in the street below and we're hungry. There are spicy smells from the nearby Moroccan restaurant. Pastilla, chicken tagine and a bottle of house wine will do nicely.

The weekend already seems too short as we breakfast in an outside café overlooking the river, ordering croissants and café au lait just like we've practised in class. Like a long together couple we wander arm in arm along the Seine in the spring sunshine, past patches of late pink blossom falling from the cherry trees. Past the Louvre and through the Jardin des

Tuileries. It's Croque Monsieur and chilled beer for lunch at a street table and then decision time. Shall we go to the Eiffel Tower or head north and climb the steps of Sacré-Cœur? See the views over Paris from the top floor of the Galeries de la Fayette? There's a silent understanding between us that we need to go back to our room.

Daniel has a plan for supper tonight. The bistro is tucked down an alleyway that smells of Paris sewers. This tiny wood panelled place is famous for its traditional cooking and it's packed and busy. The waiters seem as old as their bistro tables and shuffle about in white jackets with waiterly efficiency.

'Une coupe de champagne garçon s'il vous plaît.' Daniel's French sounds very London. We share sizzling plates of frogs legs and escargots and laugh at our tourist choices. Then a wooden board of poulet roti with a mountain of matchstick frites and salade frisée. Fraises des bois and crème fraîche and we're done. No, two glasses of Armagnac. Merci.

Daniel is missing when I wake in our soft, soft bed with the sun streaming in through the balcony windows. The sumptuous pillows smell of patchouli. Where is he? Bang, bang – he's opened our door, carrying a tray.

'Continental breakfast Madame – croissants, butter, apricot jam and a hot pot of coffee. Compliments of the concierge.'

This is perfect. A perfectly starched and ironed tray cloth on a perfectly laid tray. Full marks in my housecraft exam.

Bugger it. This man is perfect. Just look at him. No more sightseeing. Let's just stay in this perfectly beautiful room until it's time to make the sad, sad journey to the tiny airport to board a tiny plane that flips over the Channel on our journey home.

Goodnight to Daniel. Unattainably perfect. Married and mortgaged and not mine.

Next week it's the half term holiday from school and a break for my French class. It feels like a long time before we'll get to sit next to each other again.

Summer Half Term 1973

Summer Half term 1973

Half term and my Mini Traveller heads up the M1 to Kettering. It's asparagus time in my grandmother's garden and she's written a letter telling me to hurry up before it bolts. Grandma's huge asparagus patch bursts with green shoots in springtime and by October the unpicked stems have changed into beautiful feathered fronds with red berries which she uses in her autumn flower arrangements. Grandma has a special asparagus knife that she sharpens on a particular paving stone on her garden path. We pick shoots of all sizes – thin, thick and even ones with their tips bursting open.

'Cut the spears just below the ground, Jenny – don't snap them off, it just wastes the bit underneath.'

We boil the green stems in her largest aluminium pan, drain and pile them onto her favourite blue patterned meat serving dish. And there are loads.

'Pick one up with your fingers and dip it in this melted butter.' Grandma would never use margarine.

Asparagus is the most luxurious flavour of her garden which is just springing into life. I often wonder why my wee stinks so strongly after these asparagus sessions but I've never asked grandma if hers smells the same. A question just too personal for a lady brought up in the Edwardian age.

Before I leave she shows me a page from her local *Evening Telegraph* that she reads avidly every night, especially the births and obituaries which feed into local gossip.

'They are saying that Princess Anne is getting engaged soon you know. She's two years younger than you.'

I know, I know grandma, but it's easier for royalty. They don't have to go on the pick up in wine bars or dabble with married men. Well, Princess Margaret did.

Daniel has left a letter on the hall table in my bedsit house when I get back. We'll meet at the Camden Roundhouse as he's got a spare ticket to a music gig for an up and coming rock band and his wife doesn't want to go. Seems they don't like the same music. Daniel tells me of the famous bands he's heard there – David Bowie, Pink Floyd and Arthur Brown who nearly set the place on fire.

We meet outside this funny round building that was once a place for turning trains around on their journeys from London to Birmingham. Tonight's performance is a very loud, smoky rock concert with a band whose name I can't remember and whose songs it's too noisy to hear. We wave our arms and shout but I understand why this stuff wasn't to his wife's taste. He has to rush back home which makes me feel rather lonely and single.

How to gut a fish

The exam lot is not in school – they're out on study leave. Ha ha! It's a year before my fourth year classes take their exams and I'm pleased so many are becoming enthusiastic, skilled cooks. The usual scattering of students who hate school is still a nuisance as they've discovered that by disrupting lessons they get suspended for a week which gives them an escape route.

Today it's my fish lesson but the fishmonger seems worried. I ask him why his prices for cod and haddock have increased. The only way I can afford white fish for my lessons is to buy Birds Eye frozen chunks from the supermarket freezer.

'Haven't you heard of the Cod War?'

No, I'm much too busy trying to change my single status to watch TV or listen to the radio.

'Icelandic patrol boats have stopped our trawlers from fishing in their waters. They've extended their fishing grounds and now our government is sending in three Royal Navy frigates to protect our fishermen. And our ships have got guns and rocket missiles.'

So there. This could put the kibosh on our great British Fish and Chip shops if the Royal Navy lets off their rockets. Seems a bit extreme just for a few Atlantic cod.

We hardly ate any fish at home. Maybe it's because we live in the Midlands, in the middle of the country, far away from the sea. Our Friday night fish and chips from our cousin's Kettering chip shop was the limit of my fish knowledge. The newspaper print came off onto the chips if you sprinkled on too much vinegar and my mother would put everything, still wrapped in newspaper, to heat up in the oven if we took too long to get back.

In London a new fish is on the menu – Trout with Almonds has become a speciality dish. My show-off friends who have a table in their flats are serving it at their posh dinner parties. You just shove the whole trout in the oven with a dob of margarine and wrap it up in foil, then serve it scattered with toasted almonds. Guests must repress their distaste at removing the whole head and fins and piling the bits on a bone graveyard in the centre of the table. It's easy peasy compared with the fishy dishes like Coquilles St Jacques and prawn cocktail that I made when Mark and I had elaborate parties.

And yes, I know scallops and prawns aren't fish. But our bible, *O Level Cookery,* says there are three groups of fish – white, oily, and crustaceans. So scallops and prawns are fish.

They are ready on the stools and I've got a surprise in store.

'Class – you need to learn these three groups of fish for your exam. White, oily and crustaceans.'

'Eels, Miss – which are they?'

Terry is a homework absconder and a shopping basket refusenik. He's been eating his cooking in my room, against Mr Lewes' instructions.

'Eels aren't fish, Terry – they're ... eels so don't count for this lesson.'

Eels. Hideous, bony, thick skinned lumps of slimy, jellied things, served cold in a bowl at Manze's in Walthamstow High Street. A 'much-hallowed east end delicacy'. I wonder how long that shop will last.

Many of my boys are expert fishermen, and catch eels, carp, pike and tench from the Lee Valley fishing lakes. I'm pleased they put them all back when they've finished.

Now for the surprise. The wrapped up newspaper on my demonstration table hides a glistening fresh herring.

The newspaper sticks to the damp fish scales, and as I unwrap it there's a collective gulp of horror.

There are more fish hidden in the cupboard – surprise. The fishmonger has delivered a herring for each of them.

'Do you know why I've chosen herrings today, class?'

Silence. They're studying their stool legs.

'They're cheap and there are lots of ways to cook them like soused herring.'

I hold my herring up by its tail for the class to inspect.

A weak gelatinous strand of blood slides from its mouth.

'Class, how do you know if it's fresh?'

Sandra makes a retching noise and covers her mouth as if to hold in sick.

'Look at its eyes Miss, and squeeze it.'

'Thanks, Terry – look at its clear, shiny eyes.'

The herring's eyes are dull and bloodshot. It's had enough.

'And what about its gills?'

I prise open the scaly, gill-covering flap hiding rows of red fronds, open its jaw and make a gasping sound. The girls looked shocked. Surely this fish is dead?

'Gills should be bright red and its body firm. Learn for the EXAM.'

Ah ha. Is that the reason for this smelly, fishy lesson?

'Ugh, Miss – chop its head off.'

Sandra folds her arms. Her stubbornness reminds me of Carol, who should be revising for her exam. Should, yes in my dreams.

'Class, look at this lovely fish – silvery scales and perky fins.'

I make a swift slit of the belly from bottom hole to head, and intestines, blood vessels and liver spill onto the chopping board.

'Here is the roe – mine is a female with eggs. Female is hard roe, male is soft roe. We'll know the sex of your fish when you open it.' They like to talk about sex.

'And this is the swim bladder which keeps it afloat.'

The long silvery sac has a bubble of air which I squeeze backwards and forwards.

They peer at the saucer as it passes round the group.

Deep down they rather like these barmy lessons. While their friends sit in a boring Maths class, they have tales of gore and ghastliness.

'You'll never guess what we did today. We sexed a herring.'

'Chop off the head, clip the fins, press it flat and remove the backbone. Roll it up with onion and we'll souse it.'

'Scouse it Miss?'

My Midland accent probably sounds Liverpudlian to them.

No, souse it Paul.'

'Have you ever met the Beatles, Miss?' Paul is probing into my private life. I'm not telling him that Paul McCartney is my favourite, even if they share a name.

'Actually, Paul, I saw them live at Hammersmith Odeon in 1965. Everyone screamed and climbed over their seats to get to the stage. Except for me. We didn't hear any of their songs. The screaming was too loud and people fainted and were carried off on stretchers.'

My status has increased from cookery teacher to mildly interesting human being. The Beatles are pop history, the group stopped playing together in 1970 and they haven't been in the pop charts for months but once upon a time Miss saw them play live music.

'Class let's get on or we will never finish.'

My fish is rolled, its tail pushed through its back into a fan, then into a Pyrex dish with peppercorns and vinegar, covered with foil and cooked until soft.

As they return to their places, Cynthia hands out the secret herring stash. Sandra is stuck on her stool.

'Miss, I'm telling yer, I ain't doing that.'

'OK Sandra, sit at my desk and read this book.'

I hand over my copy of Fish Cookery by the Ministry of Food which seems to be written by an out of work speechwriter from Churchill's war room. I point a fishy finger to the paragraph for study -

'We are fortunate to be an island race. Our coasts have many fine harbours for ships, and the seas round our shores teem with fish. While many nations with little or no seaboard would give much to have this valuable supply for its larder, we do not always take the trouble to use it as we might.'

That should shut her up.

The rest of the class quietly fillets their fish with a few 'Yuks' and 'This is disgusting' and soon a vinegary, fishy smell wafts from the ovens.

On my demonstration table are two plates – one of beige, slimy male roes and the other, perky female eggs. There seems to be an equal balance of the sexes in the dead herring world, just like my cookery classes.

They fill my bins with fish heads, guts, swim bladders and backbones. I hope they have enjoyed my biology-cookery lesson but I fear that only a few will return to collect their soused herrings at home time.

Tonight is our French class and I hope I'm not smelling of fish. Daniel and I sit together and join the group for a drink in the pub but he leaves early. Says he's got urgent things to sort before the morning. At the weekend on a trip to Liberty's in Regent Street I bought a bottle of Je Reviens perfume. For its name really – Je

Reviens means I'll be back. The assistant says it has notes of amber, musk and cloves – an earthy reminder of patchouli. Since our shouty, jumpy, noisy night at the Roundhouse Daniel's not asked to meet up. I wonder if his wife knows about us.

The practical exam

June 1973 brings the final judgement of my teaching skills. The Cookery Practical Exam. Sixty students have to cook an elaborate, edible meal, with a hot drink, flower arrangement and other silly exam tasks that they throw at us. This feat takes place over several days as each student is allowed their own cooker and sink.

These are the tasks they have to choose from:

'Cook a two course lunch for 4 people and prepare an evening dish for someone coming back from a fishing trip. Clean a pair of muddy football boots.'

'Prepare a hot breakfast for a family of four who is going out for the day. Make a packed lunch and some cakes and a drink for them to take with them. Wash and starch some napkins.'

'Prepare an evening meal for a family with a teenage girl. Make sure that the meal is rich in iron and calcium. Bake some pasties for a packed lunch. Wash and iron a shirt.'

The exam lasts two and a half hours and they must keep to time, produce edible dishes and present on a nicely laid table.

Mr Shield the fund donor has agreed that the school will cover the exam cost and I must provide all the ingredients. For days they've been bringing in their shopping lists and we've checked and added stuff if they've forgotten. Imagine the howls of dismay if the minced beef for their Cornish pasties was missing.

The exam starts and I switch from helpful teacher to THE EXAMINER and march round the room with my clipboard, watching my students peel and chop vegetables, prepare pastry, bake cakes, biscuits and bread. I take off marks for sloppy cooking skills, messy worktops and general flustered bumbling.

They've had lots of practice at learning what loses marks. I peek over shoulders, open up saucepan lids, bend down to peer into ovens, and rootle in the rubbish bin for food wastage.

They've had warnings during exam rehearsals of things that lose marks.

'Turn the pan handle in – someone could knock over the boiling water.'

'Don't cut off all that potato skin – use a potato peeler.'

'Use your fingertips to rub the pastry fat into the flour – you are squeezing it into a soggy lump.'

'Don't throw bits of pastry away – make jam tarts or cream horns – no wastage.'

'Don't peel the apple with the cook's knife.'

'If you lick your food I won't taste it.'

Privately I love licking. Fluffy margarine and sugar, beaten to pale creaminess for Victoria sandwich is my favourite. Foamy, whisked eggs and sugar for Swiss roll comes a close second.

They know the rigid rules to distinguish savoury and sweet dishes. Savoury flans and cheesy scones are cooked and cut with PLAIN rings and cutters.

Sweet tarts and lemon meringue pies must have FLUTED edges. These are the RULES laid down in some Victorian kitchen and they are not to be BROKEN.

On a visit to Sainsbury's I notice their savoury quiche has a fluted pastry case. I'm shocked at this unforgivable sin committed by food product developers.

And they know the d'oyley rules – plain for savouries and frilly for sweet scones and cakes. One mark lost for the wrong choice and a scowl from me.

On exam day they work in silence. Except for emergencies.

'I feel sick Miss.'

'Just keep on cooking Liz – we can't waste these ingredients.'

'I've dropped my eggs on the floor, Miss.'

'Bert, here's a cloth – clear up and start again.'

I only help if there is real danger.

'Tim – take that tea towel off the top of your cooker. It's about to catch fire.'

'Please Miss, it was an accident.'

I press my finger to my lips. No speaking, no excuses, this is the real test.

'OK, class you have twenty minutes to go.'

Gasps of panic. They must present everything that's finished. No finished dish = no mark.

'I've burnt the cake, Miss.'

'Alice cut off the black bits and cover it with icing.'

'My chocolate mousse isn't set.'

'Ray, stick it in the freezer, quick.'

They scurry round the room, tarting up the dishes with garnishes of parsley for savoury and sticky glacé cherries and angelica diamonds for sweet desserts.

Suddenly it is over. 'Time's up – present your food.'

Amazing pies with crisp, golden pastry appear hot from the oven.

Steaming dishes of perfectly cooked cabbage and carrots sprinkled with chopped parsley and topped with a knob of melting margarine.

Soft mounds of creamy mashed potato, decorated with a sprig of parsley.

Pineapple upside down cake glistening with glacé cherries and rings of tinned pineapple served with a jug of creamy Bird's Custard.

And a pot of tea with a strainer, jug of milk, sugar bowl and matching Beryl Ware cups and saucers.

And a rose in a polished vase.

And a clean pair of football boots. Or a starched tray cloth.

They scramble out leaving sinks heaving with dirty plates, bowls, burnt pans and sticky baking trays.

Now for my marking session.

All dishes have to be tasted and my face remains deadpan. The students peer through the classroom windows watching for my reactions. When I tasted an unusually sweet beef stew, I realised the student used icing sugar instead of flour to thicken the sauce. The dish was inedible so no marks. I think she saw me screw up my face in horror.

There are other ways I test their cooking. Are the bread rolls crisp? Is the shepherd's pie well seasoned? Are the vegetables cooked but not overcooked? Has the egg custard curdled? Is the cake thoroughly baked?

I poke and prod, slice, taste and appreciate. It is delicious. They have done me proud.

The marking is over and they surge in to photograph and fuss. Friends come in to congratulate but mainly to eat. Then pack up, wash up, and leave with a wave and 'Thanks Miss – I enjoyed that.'

I have taught them to cook and they have learnt well.

Silly fussy salad

Here in east London it's summertime and the season for salads. When the days are warm you don't need a hot meal – or so I'm told. In the classroom we don't use exotic things like avocados or alfalfa from my Soho shops. The local greengrocers display cucumbers, radishes, tomatoes and lettuce and that's it. When I teach them salad we fiddle about and make elaborate plates of over fussed vegetables. Radishes become roses, tomatoes turn into lilies, cucumber is stripped and scissored, celery made into curls and spring onions are converted into tassels. Nothing is served simply. Every item is mauled and prepared, plated and primped. And if we can stuff it we do – stuffed eggs, stuffed tomatoes, stuffed cucumber.

Salads are not tossed in French dressing. We serve them with a jug of salad cream and you help yourself.

I can hear my mother's words.

'We don't need those French people to show us how to cook.'

Lettuce from my mother's garden was a choice of crunchy Cos or the sweet leaves of Little Gem. The greengrocers near the school send us floppy, round lettuces with limp, tasteless leaves. All fur coat and no knickers I call it. The lettuce looks OK but it's naked nothingness. No wonder students hate it.

I dump the droopy lettuces in the butler's sink full of ice cold water to perk it up. Examiners don't like this as they tell me the Vitamin C will seep into the water. But we've got nothing else.

So today for our salad we're arranging a plate of colourful salad vegetables with some stuffed eggs. It's a task to learn for the EXAM. I provide all the ingredients, so everything must be the same size and quality.

'His tomato's bigger than mine Miss.'

Liz always protests about the size of my offerings. I wonder if she'll get a job for a campaign organization, or work in local politics.

'I don't want them radishes – they've got weevils.'

Bert likes the best quality produce and might grow up to be a greengrocer.

Hard boiled eggs are our protein food today. In truth we can't afford anything else. I arrive early and boil 25 eggs in a huge saucepan of water, then plunge them into a sink of cold water to keep the yolks yellow.

'I want a brown egg Miss – me Nan says brown eggs are best.'

'Liz, I've told you, the colour doesn't matter. You don't eat the shell.'

Liz glowers. Nan has stern things to say about my cookery lessons.

She's told Liz she must have hot food at lunchtime and Liz handed me a note from Nan explaining that this salad can't be eaten as it is cold, so can Liz make a sponge cake for tea instead.

Pete, the history teacher, is buying Liz's egg salad for his supper so I'll remind her to wash her hands before cooking, despite Nan's saying that a bit of dirt never hurt anyone.

I show them how to peel off the egg shell – if the eggs are too fresh, the shell sticks to the white. There's no date on the eggs or the egg boxes, so freshness relies on the float-in-water test.

I scoop out the hard yolk and mash it with salad cream – yum.

'Spoon this back into the egg, or use a piping bag and put it back into the egg like this.'

I pipe an impressive, golden swirl and sprinkle red paprika on top. It looks like the ones sold in my Hampstead deli.

Vegetable fiddling is next. Tomatoes are cut into lilies with pointed edges, and filled with salad cream and cottage cheese – a new ingredient on our shop shelves.

Radishes make roses and sliced spring onions become tassels. This fussed over veg is dunked into freezing water to open up and lose its nutrients.

They want to get on.

'OK – eggs then salad – we'll do the lettuce later.'

'Can I have more tomato instead of this green stuff?'

Eggs are twirled and salad primped.

The lettuce, radish and spring onions need patting dry with a tea towel. No fancy salad spinners here.

'Place in colourful sections on a plate, put your eggs on top, sprinkle with mustard and cress and serve with a jug of SALAD CREAM.'

What a fuss for something which could be chopped, tossed and served in a bowl. Like those French people do.

The Final Theory Exam

It's exam time and the bright June sunshine makes study hard. Students snooze on the grass banks by the school playing fields using open textbooks as a face shade. Nearby, energetic teachers, who are now free of classes, are playing jolly games of tennis and letting out screams of 'Good shot' which must surely be distracting if you want to revise. But students could work at home or go to the school library. Surely more sensible than sunshine?

During exam time the school corridors are quiet and serious. Jim sets up the hall with long rows of desks and for weeks students have been filing in looking worried and ill prepared. Anxious teachers wait outside the hall for a preview of the paper and either pump the air with triumph or shake their heads wearily.

The dark haired boy-man from the January mocks passed by my room one afternoon carrying his exam stuff on his way to the exam hall. He glanced through my window and I gasped at his young handsomeness. They say that a cat can look at a king. And I feel like a cat with no cream.

Now it's the turn for my exam papers. Cookery exams are always last. They're the hardest too. My lot has to pass both a practical test and a theory paper and some are so poor at writing that I wonder how they will cope. I feel like a mother hen as I wish them 'good luck' as they amble in to find their desk. This exam matters so much to all of us but I'm not confident of success when I've had so little time to teach them. Before the double hall doors close and our fate is sealed, Mr Lewes hands me the exam paper and tells me that Carol and some of the boys have not turned up.

I make a quiet return to my room and lock the door. They've got two hours and have to select the questions they will answer so they must read through the whole paper.

If this exam mentions a bloody housewife in their questions I will scream.

And here it comes.

'How will a housewife lessen the danger of food poisoning in the home?'

And

'Suggest two dinners for a housewife who does her own cooking and shopping.'

The shout just comes out, suddenly, angrily. No! No! And then the scream. A passerby might think it's an attack but it's my total rage that in the 1970s some examiner still thinks that housewives do everything in the home and are the only sex that knows about making meals when I've got a group of boys in the hall answering her – I assume it is a woman – stupid questions. This has to change. The exam board is getting a letter from me. Why do they keep asking about housewives in cookery exams? What about the other half of the population – men? What about my boys and their future shared partnerships? Do they ask questions about husbands in theory exams for metalwork and woodwork? If not why not? Aggh. I'm off to the staffroom for a smoke.

My classes come into my room after the exam ends.

'It was alright Miss. They asked about cooking for an invalid and we had to draw a sheep and mark in the joints.'

'And I wrote about what a housewife should know about food values and meal planning.'

Oh, Bert. How I want this cookery teaching world to change.

The school flat

At the end of the corridor beyond my cookery rooms is the school flat. In the past it's been a storeroom, a sick room, and then She Who Ran Away reclaimed it as part of her empire. Some years ago the government decided that housecraft and domestic science were useful subjects to make girls into good housewives and learn to run a home. Thousands of housecraft flats were built or old rooms reclaimed in schools around the country.

No one lives in my school flat so it is never dirty.

No one bathes in the turquoise bath, or flushes the turquoise toilet or sleeps in the hard single bed.

No one reads by the electric fire, puts their clothes in the bedside cupboard, or skids on the rug on the lino floor.

My school flat is like a tiny home. The one large room has a dining and sitting area, a bed, a small kitchen and a separate bathroom with toilet. It's bigger than my bedsit and there were times on stormy winter evenings when I thought I might stay and not take the long, wet drive in my Mini Traveller to a cold, lonely bedsit room. But the school is locked at night and I reckon I'd be spooked staying in this dismal place.

Furniture and china suppliers in the 1950s must have rubbed their hands with glee when the housecraft flats needed stocking as they're all equipped with the same stuff. My flat is furnished with imitation G-Plan-style furniture, a sideboard with tapered spindly legs, a foldaway dining table, a set of six thin-legged chairs and plenty of place mats to protect the precious, overpolished, veneered wood surfaces from stains. The narrow single bed has one pillow, a thin mattress topped with a precisely mitred, tucked in sheet, and is covered with another sheet, a pastel green cellular blanket and a dark green woven cotton throw. Green is not my colour and it makes this flat feel like a gloomy garden cave.

Someone has brought in a saggy, red upholstered armchair with broken seat springs, and hung a Boot's print of the Chinese Girl above the single bar electric fire which emits so little heat it is no wonder the Chinese Girl turned blue.

The flat is used by my Housecraft CSE students to learn how to clean a bathroom, polish furniture, Hoover carpets, lay a table and make a bed. I send the girls off in pairs to compare the merits of Vim and Johnson's furniture polish, and practise that famous toilet cleaning ditty 'Flush, brush, flush the brush and flush.'

The trouble is, I'm teaching boys and girls, and cleaning a school flat in the 1970s does not appeal to any of us. The flat is out of sight, down a corridor, in a room with a bed and boys can't be trusted. In our enforced sex education lessons they tell me they know it all and I don't want them in the flat finding out more.

The sooner we stop this stupid Housecraft exam the better.

Meantime we use the flat to serve a meal and lay the table with freshly ironed tablecloths, napkins and cutlery.

Quiet girls in the class are chosen to write lunch invitations to their favourite teachers with a copy of the menu and the price. The boys that I teach can't be trusted with this task. They'd get into mischief of some sort.

This is the summer lunch menu which the girls prepare:

Melon boats, served with a twist of orange, glacé cherry and a sprinkling of ground ginger
Quiche Lorraine with coleslaw and piped potatoes
Fruit salad with a jug of cream

Fresh coffee (made with instant Maxwell House) or tea.

Teachers like getting these lunch invitations and some bring a bottle of wine to celebrate. The girls make attentive waitresses – water and wine are poured, napkins spread, plates served, cleared and washed. The teachers' lunch money helps to eke out my food funds and we end up with extra ingredients like cream to use in our cooking. Kind teachers send a thankyou note and remember to pay. Forgetful ones don't get invited again.

It's the last night of my French evening class and our last drink in the pub before the summer break. Maybe we'll meet up over the holidays and some have plans for trips to France to show off conversations such as 'Où est le camping?' and 'Donnez moi plus de vin.' For the last fortnight Daniel hasn't shown any interest in seeing me after class and he hasn't turned up tonight. I can't phone or write a letter. Married men don't share their home phone number or address.

But the weekend's going to be fun. I meet friends at Hyde Park and we drift over to Kensington Market to twirl amongst the vintage clothes and silk scarves. A fairyland of treasures and fashions. One smell lingers more than the sweaty crowds and

Afghan coats – patchouli oil. Just a tiny dab from a brown bottle triggers memories. A smooth, earthy, strong fragrance that really suits a man's skin. Now the group is off for more shopping at Lee Bender's Bus Stop and to float around Biba's ostrich feathers and try on the large floppy hats, before heading for tea and cakes at Fortnum and Mason in Piccadilly. London has so much to offer. My Hampstead friends are having a party tonight and perhaps Mark will be there.

Prawn cocktail

We never ever cook with prawns, shrimps, crabs or lobsters in the classroom. They're too expensive for everyday food, and remain a treat for those who can afford to eat out.

Cockles, winkles and whelks are really popular in east London, sold on fish stalls outside busy pubs and squirted with brown vinegar from a rather grubby white plastic bottle. The muscley flesh of these weird sea creatures is peppered with crunchy sand and small stones, and more than I can bear to chew over.

Mark told me tales of his summer holiday jobs on the cockle boats that go out into the Thames estuary dredging the shellfish from the mud. He had a posher job harvesting oysters, boarding the boat from the end of Southend pier, travelling along the coast to Paglesham and collecting oysters from the rows of oyster beds along the coastline. These delicacies were mainly shipped to London but there was a thriving local trade at an oyster stall that he ran outside the Kursaal Amusement Park on Southend seafront. Day trippers had a ride on the big dipper and then tucked into a half dozen shucked oysters that he opened with his special knife. 'A really cheap treat' he told me, 'but there were times when I had to wash off the blood when I cut my hand opening the shells.'

He sometimes got into play fights with the chaps on the jam doughnut stall next door – they aimed their squirty jam and doughnut dough at him and he retaliated with oyster shells and mucky shellfish water.

When we lived together in our London flat we'd sometimes travel down to meet his family outside The Crooked Billet pub in Old Leigh and sit at the sea edge with a pint of beer, eating tiny plates of cockles from the bustling fish stalls overlooking the estuary. Fond memories.

At last weekend's party in Hampstead, Mark turned up with our other friends and we settled into an easy chat. We've been together for so long and it felt comfortable to be friends with him, so we'll meet again.

Thankfully my students don't need to know about shellfish for the EXAM, and our textbook shares my dislike.

'The flesh of shellfish is considerably less digestible than that of white and oily fish, and is not universally popular – e.g. crabs, lobsters, prawns, mussels, winkles, etc.'

This daft comment needs striking out with a red pen when I get round to it. The author should visit Old Leigh cockle sheds on a busy weekend. Gourmet food lovers of freshly cooked lobster and crabs would be very surprised to read that these delicacies are 'universally unpopular.' I need to write my own textbook.

Prawn cocktail is a favourite starter dish of the seventies especially in Berni Inns where it's served in a large wine glass on a bed of chopped lettuce, with an unshelled prawn dangling over the rim. The wine glass comes on a saucer with a frilly d'oyley with quarters of brown bread and butter, crusts removed. It's the d'oyley that bothers me. Don't Berni Inns know the d'oyley rules? Plain for savoury, frilly for sweet.

When I worked as a waitress in Wicksteed Park, prawn cocktail was a lunchtime favourite. The chef had huge glass jars of pink Heinz Marie Rose sauce that he'd mix with the prawns. The sauce was made from salad cream and tomato ketchup, which we had to mix up for him when the jar ran out.

My favourite description of prawn cocktail comes from H. E.

Bates, a Northamptonshire author who wrote his famous books, *The Darling Buds of May* about Pop Larkin and his family. In his story, Pop and Ma Larkin visit their neighbour's house for dinner and Pop thinks everything looks 'trés snob'. His posh meal starts with a prawn cocktail and he describes a tiny glass dish filled with a few prawns, a soapy pink sauce and a dead prawn hanging over the edge searching for its mates that he could eat with two digs of his teaspoon.

My grandfather said he taught Herbert Bates in his Science lessons at Kettering Grammar School in the 1920s. I was desperate to ask more questions but by this time my grandfather was in the twilight zone and found grandchildren irritating. H.E. Bates's books depict the Northamptonshire countryside where I grew up, and his prawn cocktail story will stay with me forever. I'd love to know what my grandfather taught him.

The textbook offers no homework questions on crustaceans or shellfish so I scratch my own chalky words on the black roller board.

'Visit your local cockle stall and find out where they get their shellfish from. Make a list of all the fish, shellfish and crustaceans that they sell.'

If they are lucky, I might tell them my story about Mark and his cockles next week but I need to ask him first. I've got a suspicion that cockle means something rude in Cockney rhyming slang, so I need to be careful as there are some expert local linguists in my classes.

The picnic

Very few students eat lunch at school. They would rather nip to the chippy at the end of the road and buy a bag of fried, battered bits or get a '99 ice cream from the Mr Whippy van, which belches diesel fumes outside the school gates.

Today we're learning about picnics and packed lunches. We might be asked these kinds of questions:

Prepare a packed meal for two hungry school boys on a bicycle tour.

Prepare a packed meal for two schoolgirls to take on a long train journey.

Bah! I can't imagine any of my students going on a bicycle tour or taking a long train journey. They like to be driven around by car.

The July days are so hot and many staff are teaching lessons outside so I'm joining in. I have planned a fun surprise for this lovely summer's day.

'We're going to make this picnic and take it down to the school field and eat together.

I've got permission, so we'll go as part of the lesson.'

They're appalled. A picnic. School field. With their teacher. I must be joking.

I get Terry to read from our textbook. It's really a trick to quieten them.

'Packed meals are required by workers unable to obtain midday meals at their places of employment and for picnics. Balance the packed meal as carefully as the main meal. There is always a danger of including too great a proportion of carbohydrates. The day of the traditional sandwich is now almost over – avoid too much bread.' It carries on...

'Make the fullest use of the large variety of plastic equipment now available. Portable cruets should be added to every picnic and always supply some sort of drink.'

Something's got to be done about these stupid books with their bread avoidance and cruet requirements.

I'm moaning in the staffroom about my lack of plastic boxes when Jackie says I can stock up at her auntie's Tupperware party.

'She's got lots of lovely stuff. Last week I bought a thing on a swirly stick with trays that swing round and hold cocktail nibbles.'

I've never been to a cocktail party and wonder if I need a special frock.

'Jackie, I have to buy everything from Central Supplies. Get your auntie to send me a catalogue.'

I'd secretly love an invite to auntie's naughty knickers and nightie parties that Jackie chuckles about. Perhaps I could buy something alluring for an imaginary date. Never mind. We'll wrap our picnic bits in foil.

This is our picnic menu for the school field:

Scotch eggs, Tomato and cucumber chunks, Rock cakes, Freshly squeezed orange juice.

We roast the Scotch eggs. No deep fat fryer in my room. It's much too dangerous. Then bake the rock cakes, cut up the tomatoes and cucumber, and finally squeeze the oranges. The boys take the tablecloths and jugs of orange juice and glasses and the girls carry picnic baskets with salt and pepper cruets just as the book says. Boys don't carry baskets, so there is no point asking. While the girls sit quietly tucking into warm Scotch eggs, even the hungriest boy is missing.

'Where are they Sally?'

'They said they wouldn't be seen dead sitting here, Miss. They've probably gone to the chip shop.'

Taking students out for a picnic. Silly idea. Stay in the classroom and have done with it.

It's Friday and tonight my friends and Mark are heading for the Mixed Bathing Pond on Hampstead Heath. I've packed my swimming costume and towel, some Scotch eggs leftover from the school picnic and our friends will bring loads of Mateus Rosé and Blue Nun. The company that Mark works for has bought a little French Beaujolais brand called Piat which he's rather excited about. Says it's going to lead to big things for the future of the wine industry so he's bringing along some bottles for us to sample. I think we'll have fun on this warm summer evening.

An envelope with no stamp, delivered by hand, is addressed to me on the bedsit house hall table. It's from Daniel. His wife is leaving and wants a divorce. He's sorry not to have made contact but it's not been easy. He's looking forward to meeting up in the summer holidays. A drink? A trip to the seaside?

The last days of term

The fifth year has come back for their final goodbyes and I'm throwing a party. The lawn outside my room is filled with trestle tables and wooden benches and we've clipped down the seersucker tablecloths just in case this sunny summer day gets breezy and blows everything away. Students have raided the school gardens and filled my vases with flowers and laid the tables with my complete collection of Beryl Ware and Denby crockery. It's going to be a feast.

Cynthia's been helping me cook all morning and now we're sending out pudding bowls full of piping hot baked potatoes – yes, piping hot which is so difficult to test. She's made giant cheese and bacon quiches and I've used the Kenwood Chef to grate up cabbage and carrots to make massive bowls of coleslaw. And decanted our large jar of Branston Pickle into pudding bowls. And put out sauce boats of salad cream. They have a choice of water or wine – well just a little from huge two litre bottles of Liebfraumilch that was on offer in the supermarket. It's their last day and if we get caught for drinking alcohol it's too damn late.

The Kenwood Chef has been working overtime whipping up huge quantities of egg whites for pavlovas which are topped with a special luxury – whipped double cream. All finished with sliced strawberries and a sprinkling of icing sugar. A real summer treat.

Cynthia and I sit on my steps in the sunshine and smile contentedly at this group of happy teenagers with their new futures ahead. She tells me of her holiday plans to take her family to their summer caravan on the east coast. My six weeks ahead are empty although Mark has asked if I'll join him on his drive to Reims visiting the champagne houses.

'It's for work, you know, and they'll really look after us. There are lots of local Routiers in the region for great meals and we can stay in small hotels. My secretary can arrange it all. Then I'm planning to drive down to the south of France – we could eat Salad niçoise and drink chilled glasses of rosé wine.'

It's my only offer and certainly the best. Do the French have double rooms with single beds? I must be back by mid August to get my exam results. Carol and the boys who cooked such an excellent meal for their practical exam but didn't turn up for the theory exam will get an unclassified result. And as for the rest, who knows?

History Notes

Writing this memoir in 2021, I'm reminded that so many things were missing in the seventies. Many homes did not have a telephone – my parents didn't and there wasn't one in the rented flat or bedsit house. And of course, there were no mobile phones. It is amazing how we managed any kind of pre-booked social life.

The seventies was a time of change, but financially, times were hard. Britain dithered between imperial and metric – new decimal currency, old weights and measures, distance in miles, the temperature in Fahrenheit. New kitchen equipment was being introduced. Many homes did not have refrigerators. Chest freezers gradually became popular, as did slow cookers, pressure cookers and electric mixers.

Microwave cookers arrived in the late seventies along with ready meals, and 80% of us use microwaves in our kitchens today. The labels on food products had no list of ingredients, date marks or details of nutritional value. So we couldn't compare the quality of sausages or know the contents of a tin of soup. And we had to guess how old our fresh food was. I was guilty of keeping a very old jug of beaten egg in the fridge to glaze pastries and surprisingly my classes didn't get food poisoning.

The textbooks that we used in school described women and girls doing the cooking, but I had plenty of boys in my classes and it was not fair to use them. A *New Metric Edition of Cooking is Fun* by the Good Housekeeping Institute was printed in 1974 so at least we were cooking in grams and litres. The book, written for students of domestic science, only referred to girls doing the cooking so no progress there.

In 1979 I was asked to write a school textbook based upon the lessons in this memoir. My first textbook, *Finding Out About Food,* was published in the 1980s and went on to sell over 120,000 copies. Based on its success, my next book *Food around the World* was commissioned and I could visit the diverse groups living in London and research their authentic recipes. Since that time I have written over seventy textbooks with sales of over a million copies.

These are some updates on the stories in the book:

Spag bog

On April 1st 1957, the BBC showed a film of a family harvesting spaghetti from their spaghetti tree. Spaghetti was not an everyday food in the 1950s and many people believed the hoax was true. Many, like my family, didn't know that spaghetti was made from wheat and water. People asked the BBC for advice on how to grow the spaghetti tree and were told to put a sprig of spaghetti in a tin of tomato sauce.

During the pandemic, pasta sales soared by 15% in the UK as people stockpiled the dried pasta. Its long shelf life meant it could be stored with tins of tomatoes to make an easy store cupboard meal with some grated cheese. Spaghetti bolognese is the most popular dish in the UK today, followed by pizza which I never taught in the 1970s.

Boys don't cook

The Sex Discrimination Act of 1975 meant that boys and girls had equal access to all subjects in schools and equal opportunities when choosing practical subjects. However, studies showed that boys were discouraged from taking Home Economics by their teachers, peers and parents.

In a report on 'Gender roles and the curriculum: boys and home economics' published in 1983, Susan Johne criticised the strong female bias of the home economics textbooks and questions set for the exams. Her report showed how boys changed their minds when they discovered that so many girls took the subject and that it was considered cissy to cook.

In 1981 only 7% of boys were entered for exams in domestic subjects.

Teachers at the time were not allowed to set their own CSE home economics practical tests despite the multicultural mix in many cities.

Here are some exam questions from the time that reinforce the role of the woman as cook, caterer and cleaner for her husband and family. Remember, these questions were given to boys and girls for their practical and theory exam and I had to persuade them that it was old fashioned, but things would change.

Practical exam questions:

1. Your brother and a friend are playing football. Prepare, cook and serve a substantial meal for them on their return home. You are all going out for the evening. Iron the shirt your brother will wear and sponge and press either the skirt or trousers that you will wear.
2. Your father and brother are going fishing for the day. Launder your father's sweater. Leave to dry and press it if it dries in time. Make some meat pasties or pies and pack up with salad and fruit and a flask of coffee for their picnic meal. Cook and serve a substantial two course dinner ready for their return.

Theory exam question:

1. Suggest two dinners for a housewife who does her own cooking and shopping. a) a dinner cooked quickly on her return from

shopping, b) a dinner which can mainly be left cooking while she is out.

In 2019 the GCSE entries for Food Preparation and Nutrition, Home Economics and Hospitality and Catering were 18,506 Male, 35,063 Female (34%,66%) so it's changed a bit.

Wearing trousers

In the 1970s the dress code for women teachers in the London region did not allow us to wear trousers at work. We wore skirts or dresses with tights or stockings – bare legs were only allowed if you were a game's teacher. In 1969, when Mick Jagger married Bianca, she wore a trouser suit – a shocking new fashion choice. I too chose a trouser suit for my going away outfit after my wedding, which my family also found strange.

She Who Ran Away

The things I left outside my room for people to take are now on sale on eBay as vintage kitchen equipment: Iron griddle pan, £40; French aluminium fish kettle, £40; 12 hole bun tin, £16; 4 cream horn tins, £40; mince pie tin, £20.

What's in a name?

Nigel Slater in his memoir *Toast – The Story of a Boy's Hunger* – seemed frustrated that his domestic science teacher Miss Adams took so long to teach him cooking. He was part of the name change when cookery became home economics, and his teacher praised his Victoria Sandwich which 'rose like a dream' and had a perfect 'crumb'.

In 1990 the subject changed its name to Food Technology. This meant students had to learn about the industrial production of food products and make a food product that could be sold to a target group.

In 2020 the names began to change again. My 2021 Survey of Food Teachers found that 62% wanted to call their subject food and nutrition, 33% were calling it food, 2% home economics, 2% hospitality and 1% food technology, so the confusion carries on.

Discipline matters

Caning was abolished in 1987 in UK state schools.

A survey of ILEA schools in 1976-1977 showed that one in five girls was caned at least once that year.

Teachers still have legal powers to use reasonable force to remove disruptive students.

Going metric

The metric system started in France and was adopted in other European countries during the 19th century. Britain announced it would adopt metric units in 1965. In 2021 both Britain and the USA have yet to complete the changeover.

Timeline for decimalization and metrication

1971 British currency decimalised. A Government campaign to prepare the public for change.
1971 London schools adopt the metric system.
1973 UK enters EEC and commits to adopting the metric system.
1974 Metric system taught in all British schools. Metric packaging begins.
1979 The Conservative Government under Margaret Thatcher abolishes the Metrication Board.
1980 Most Commonwealth countries have completed metric conversion. Britain lags behind.

1995 All packaged goods sold in Britain have to be labelled in metric units.

2021 Milk and beer are still sold in pints.

The UK is the only country that produces recipe books with measurements in metric and imperial units – 50 years after schools started teaching it.

In 2021 in supermarkets, milk is still sold in pint bottles and beer in pubs is sold in pint glasses.

Many of the students I was teaching from the 1970s would be over sixty years old so most of the population must have discovered metric measures by now.

The Governor's tea

In the sixties I spent many days and nights in my holidays working as a waitress at Wicksteed Park Pavilion, Kettering. In the winter it had a massive ballroom which was laid with long tables for Hunt Balls and other worthy causes. My working outfit was a black dress with long sleeves, a white, lacy apron and a frilly waitress head thing that tied around my head. The apron and the head thing used to be washed and starched but we picked a black dress from the rail when we arrived at work and tried to avoid those that stank of sweat and had food stains down the front.

Wicksteed Park was created by Charles Wicksteed who ran an engineering company that made the most fabulous playground equipment. He created his park in 1921 with leisure facilities for local people including refreshment areas, a lake, a small railway and an exciting water shute. As a child, I was the champion swinger on the very tall swings in the massive playground area and could work my swing up really high then jump off onto the tarmac. Fortunately, my parents never came to check on this extremely dangerous hobby. A newspaper article said 'Wicksteed

Park – where children learnt to play' and that was true for me. The ice cream factory opened in the fifties and you could buy scoops of Wicksteed Park ice cream from the many kiosks around the parkland. Thank goodness I never got stuck working in one of those.

Angel Delight

Angel Delight was launched in the UK in 1967 by Bird's, the company that made the custard powder. By the 1970s sales had doubled – perhaps because food teachers like myself used it for our Convenience Food lessons. We were told that it encouraged children to drink more milk as it had to be added to the dessert, but water mixed it up just as well.

In 2021, Butterscotch Angel Delight is still one of the most popular flavours. The packet says it's made with real butter but the Ingredient's List shows 'Butter Powder 1%' so the Food Chemist has been busy again creating 'Yummy tasting clouds of fluffiness' – that's the packet description, not mine.

Today you can save even more time and buy ready made pots of Angel Delight – so even more convenient than my lessons.

The cheese tasting

When I was writing this memoir, I puzzled why I included Caerphilly in my cheese tastings as an English cheese. And that's because it was shown on the National Dairy Councils' posters for English Cheeses which were sent to schools. Of course, I know that Caerphilly is in Wales, but why didn't they?

The National Dairy Council and the English Country Cheese Council were part of the National Milk Publicity Council, established in 1923. It aimed to promote the consumption of milk, real dairy cream and English cheese and did a lot of work in schools.

Stork margarine

Why did we only cook with margarine in the classroom?

In 1972 butter was expensive. Half a pound (250g) cost 12p. Half a pound of Stork Margarine cost 6p, so at half the price of butter, people choose margarine.

Margarine sales began to rise during World War II with butter rationing. After the war, butter was often unavailable and unaffordable to many and margarine sales took off. In 1920 Stork was registered as a brand of margarine and money was spent on advertising to increase sales. People were initially suspicious of the health benefits of margarine and unsure of its uses.

In 1954, *The Art of Home Cooking* by Stork was published and sold tens of thousands of copies. Teams of home economists demonstrated Stork at cookery events and some visited schools. I had piles of free copies of *The Art of Home Cooking* in my cookery room and we used them frequently for recipes.

Stork today is labelled as a spread because it does not have the 80% fat required to be called margarine. In the 1970s, scientists were concerned about trans fats in margarine which were linked to the hydrogenation process during manufacture. In 2000, brands removed hydrogenated fats from margarine but sales have continued to fall as consumers chose to return to natural food products like butter.

Good Housekeeping's *Cooking is Fun* (1974) used margarine in all their recipes except for buttercream icing where it was optional and I used margarine in all my 1970s school cooking and the textbooks that I wrote.

Rosehips

During World War II the Women's Institute organised rosehip collections. The rosehips were boiled in water – which destroyed much of the vitamin C – and preserved by using LOTS of sugar so the nutritional value of the syrup was poor. After the war,

Delrosa sold the syrup commercially and supplied many baby clinics throughout the UK.

This is the wartime recipe: Mince 2lb rosehips and boil with 3 pints of water. Cool then sieve through muslin to get a clear liquid. Boil to reduce to 1½ pints then add 20 oz sugar, boil again and store in sterilised bottles.

The story of Be-Ro flour

Thomas Bell set up a grocery firm in the 1880s and one of his top-selling brands was 'Bells Royal' baking powder and a self raising flour. Following the death of Edward VII, it became illegal to use the Royal name, so Bell took the first couple of letters from the brand name and invented 'Be-Ro'. In the early 1920s, plain flour was the most popular flour. Self-raising flour was more expensive.

To make self-raising flour more widely known, the company attended exhibitions and sold freshly baked scones and cakes to visitors. People wanted the recipes for home baking, so the free Be-Ro recipe book was written and handed out at the exhibitions and posted to people's homes. Some of these books were used in school.

The Loose Box

In the 1970s, London wine bars were opening all over town. Many London pubs were dingy and run down and divided into two areas – the Public Bar where the men gathered for serious drinking, and the Saloon Bar where posher people met and sat at tables. The wine bars came along in the sixties and seventies and they offered a refreshing alternative for young people to meet, eat and chat. They served cheese boards, cheese fondues, snacky things and an increasingly wide choice of good wine – and were an important pickup place for young men and women like me.

Egg Magic

The British Egg Marketing Board was set up in 1957 to buy all eggs produced in the UK, grade them to a national standard, stamp a lion on the egg as a mark of quality, and market these eggs through registered packhouses. Producers got a price for first quality eggs, and second quality and sample eggs went for industrial use. The Board deducted a levy from producers, based on the volume of egg production and this money was used for administration and to support research, education, PR and advertising. The Board closed in 1971. From 1958-68, £12 million was spent on advertising, including the famous slogan 'Go to Work on an Egg'. At that time the lion logo was considered unsuccessful as consumers did not know the quality of eggs. The lion mark was reintroduced in 1998 to reduce cases of salmonella, as the mark offered assurance that the hens had been vaccinated.

Today, commercially farmed British hens are all vaccinated against many diseases including salmonella.

On the shelf

The pressure on me to be told I was 'on the shelf' at twenty three years old was alarming. It means: 'To put aside as of no further use.' Used to describe people, projects and objects. 'A single woman beyond the average age of marriage is said to be on the shelf.' Brewers Dictionary. In the 1970s, being a single woman with no marriage prospects was a great worry for me and my friends.

Beaujolais Nouveau

In 1985, the Institut National des Appellations d'Origine (INAO) decreed that the third Thursday of November at 12.01 was the release date and time for the wine. Beaujolais Nouveau is bottled six to eight weeks after harvest and is intended for immediate drinking, slightly chilled and does not keep. My husband gave his father a bottle which he opened after 10 years and was disgusted at how awful it tasted.

I never taught chicken

So what was happening to chicken production in the seventies, and what has happened to chicken production today? The booklet, *Chicken in the Kitchen, a National Poultry Show Publication* was produced by The National Farmers Union just after the war. Its President gives a clue about why chicken was so expensive in the 1970s.

'We know that you would like to have more chickens but for the time being we are limited by the feeding stuffs available. Poultry may be a luxury to many of us, but one day we hope to make it at least an egg a day and some chicken each week for all of you.'

Sainsbury's produced a leaflet *All About Chicken* in the 1970s, which once again helped the housewife – clearly men did not do the choosing or shopping.

'You can get a reasonably sized chicken from about 7/- (35p) at Sainsbury's, as Sainsbury's are among the largest buyers of chicken in the country. Roasting chickens are marked with a blue label; boiling fowls with a red label.' It explains how to cook a whole chicken and use the leftovers, and how to use the new chicken halves and quarters on sale. Spaghetti chicken is one of the dishes, using canned spaghetti, onion and minced chicken.

In the 1960s, chickens were farmed mainly for their eggs, and when the tough, exhausted birds reached the end of their egg laying days, they were called boiling fowl and stewed and made into pies.

In the 1950s Britain produced just 1 million chickens a year – today it is over a billion.

Intensive farming methods were imported from the US and in

the late 1960s the price of chicken dropped by a third. During the late 1970s government campaigns advised people to eat less fatty, red meat and choose chicken as a leaner, healthier alternative. By the 1990s nearly a quarter of meat eaten in Britain was chicken or turkey. In 1972, the year of my memoir, chicken was still too expensive to cook in school and none of the textbooks wrote about it or asked questions in the dreaded exams so I didn't include it in my teaching.

Today chicken is the most popular meat around the world – in 2021 there were 25 billion farmed chickens. Most poultry is intensively farmed but the price of chicken is now affordable and popular.

Lamb's hearts

My students were right to claim that lamb's hearts are used to feed dogs. These are the instructions from *A Guide to Lamb's Heart for Dogs:*

Lamb's hearts can be purchased whole or raw or freeze dried.

Lamb's hearts are suitable to feed as part of a raw diet or as a highly palatable treat.

Lamb's hearts are nutritious, high in protein and full of nutrients.

OXO cubes

OXO cubes became very popular from the 1950s and there was a TV advert with Katie who cooked using OXO to make her husband happy. The catchphrase was 'OXO gives a meal man appeal' which I used to encourage the boys to cook. The adverts stopped in 1976 as life was changing and more women were going out to work and families did not regularly eat together.

From 1920 the famous OXO Tower on the south bank of the River Thames was the site of the meat company that made OXO beef stock cubes. Today you can buy OXO cubes in Beef, Chicken, Ham, Lamb and Vegetable flavours.

The day my hair caught fire

Gas cookers no longer have pilot lights inside the ovens. Gas ovens today are ignited by an electric ignition system which saves the major hazard of explosions and the danger of setting cooks alight.

Beryl Ware and D'oyleys

Wood & Sons was a large and successful earthenware manufacturer in the Stoke on Trent pottery towns of Trent and later in Burslem. The company Beryl Ware from the 1940s produced teaware, tableware, fancy earthenware and hotel ware and were hugely popular in homes, village halls, school canteens and hospitals throughout the UK as well as the nation's cookery rooms.The colours were limited by wartime restrictions and it came in three colours – mint green, jasmine and iris. The mint green coloured range that I used in school was the most popular. It was called utility earthenware and hardly ever broke despite the rough washing up done by the boys. The company closed in 1995.

Is it doilie, doily or d'oyley? Who knows but the rules for frilly d'oyleys for sweet things and plain d'oyleys for savoury became popular in the 1960s and then became the rules for catering organisations and school cookery lessons. Thank goodness they are no longer in fashion and now used to make Christmas decorations.

The Little Nipper

The Little Nipper Mousetrap was designed by the British inventor James Henry Atkinson and it was first made in 1897. He sold his mousetrap patent to Procter Brothers in 1913. The original had a wood base but it's now made of plastic and is the most successful mousetrap holding 60% of the UK mousetrap market. I visited the company's 150-exhibit mousetrap museum many years ago at its factory in Bedwas, Caerphilly and was shown the many fascinating ways to catch a mouse. The collection has been donated to St Fagans National History Museum so you can see it for yourself.

School dinners

What is Spam?

Spam was invented in 1937 and became popular as a canned food during World War II. It's made from pork and ham, salt, water, modified starch, sugar, and sodium nitrite – a preservative. It's believed that it gets its name from Spiced Ham or Specially Processed American Meat. In the 1970s, the Monty Python team did a sketch eating in a greasy spoon café where the menu was 'Spam, spam, spam, a boiled egg, spam' – a bit like my school dinners.

Is it called dinner or lunch?

A survey of a sample of 1,000 Britons found that 53% called the main evening meal dinner, 39% called it tea and 8% called it supper. In northern England 68% called the main evening meal tea, but in London, only 5% called it tea.

Colin Spencer, author of *British Food: An Extraordinary Thousand Years of History*, told me:

'If you are a member of the lower classes or live outside London and the south-east, the midday meal is called dinner and is often the main meal of the day. But for the upper classes and metropolitans, the midday meal is called lunch. In the evening, the lower classes and northerners come home from work, school or shopping and sit down to another fairly substantial meal called tea at about 6pm.'

In 2021, at midday students stay for school dinners yet at the same time other students can eat a packed lunch.

Ah! Bisto!

This was a popular phrase used on adverts for Bisto gravy powder which browns, thickens and seasons all in one go. In the adverts, two children in ragged clothes caught the smell from the cooking and said, Ah! Bisto! A phrase that we used for delicious meaty dishes.

The slop pot

In the thrifty 1970s, slow cookers became popular as more women joined the workforce. Saving money on fuel bills was also important, so cooking food all day over a light bulb was admired. A few years later, the slow cooker is used to cook the newly fashionable dish, chilli con carne, using dried red kidney beans. If cooks followed one popular recipe instructions, the dried beans were not boiled long enough for a harmful toxin, lectin, to be destroyed. The toxin can lead to sickness and diarrhoea and make you feel really poorly. Canned red kidney beans, which are safe to eat from the can, were not yet widely for sale. Dried kidney beans should be first cooked in boiling water for at least 10 minutes.

Vegetarian cooking

The Vegetarian Society was founded in 1847 and the first vegetarian hospital was opened in Ramsgate in 1846. It is amazing how little impact The Society had on the things that were taught in school cookery lessons in the 1970s. The Vegetarian Society now has its own logo that goes on food labels and its extensive website 'provides imaginative, creative and delicious vegetarian food' and resources for schools.

The Vegan Society was created in 1944 when a group of non-dairy vegetarians gave the name to describe themselves – vegan from VEGetariAN. The Society wanted to show 'that the use of animal products, such as meat, dairy, eggs, leather and wool, will be viewed as an inhumane and unsustainable practice from a much less enlightened age.'

Haldane Foods is one of the country's oldest producers of meat and dairy-free products. Their brands include names such as Realeat, Direct Foods and Granose which was established over 100 years ago. Some company products were invented by Dr John Harvey Kellogg, famous for cornflakes.

Easter Leaving

On September 1st 1972 when I started teaching at my new school, the school leaving age was raised from 15 to 16. Students that wanted to escape school and start a job were suddenly stuck which made them difficult to teach especially if they were not going to take exams. When the leaving age was raised in 1972, it meant about a third of pupils, who would previously have left, stayed in school.

The Department of Education and Science London: 1971 issued a circular.

It said that pupils would be entitled to leave school at the end of either the Easter or Summer term 1973 depending on the date of their 16th birthday.

If their 16th birthday fell between 1st September and 31st January they can leave at the end of the Easter term so don't stay through the summer term when exams are taken.

If their birthday falls between 1st February and 31st August they can leave on the Friday before the first Monday in May which also means they don't do exams.

Those whose sixteenth birthday falls on any date from 1 September 1973 to 31 January 1974 (inclusive) will stay at school until the end of the Easter term 1974 and those whose sixteenth birthday falls on any date from 1 February 1974 to 31 August 1974 (inclusive) will stay at school until the end of the Summer term 1974.

So for my next teaching year of 1973-74 the muddle continued.

The Department was happy that the teaching force had recruited sufficient numbers of teachers to deal with the extra students and increased the number of classrooms to accommodate them. In the autumn term of 1974 my second cookery room was opened.

Using leftovers

Food had to be heated until it was piping hot and this term has now been defined and the temperature of reheated food is carefully measured with a temperature probe. These are the rules – always reheat food until it is piping hot all the way through – above 75°C for at least 30 seconds. It is unhygienic to stick your finger in to test the temperature as recommended in some recipe books.

Drinka Pinta Milka Day

'Drinka Pinta Milka Day' was a national Milk Marketing Board campaign that started in 1958 and ran for many years. I'm glad they didn't use these other slogans when I was teaching. 'Is your man getting enough?' and 'Milk's gotta lotta bottle' would have led to embarrassing classroom questions.

How to gut a fish

There is only confirmed death during the Cod War. That was an Icelandic engineer who was accidentally killed in the Second

Cod War while he was repairing damage on the Icelandic patrol boat. In 2021 fishing rules and fishing limits are once again in the news.

Silly fussy salad

When I was teaching in the 1970s, we put salad cream into lots of recipes such as stuffed eggs and coleslaw and served it in a posh jug or sauce boat with a meal.

Salad cream was the first brand developed in 1925 by Heinz for the UK market and sales increased during rationing as it livened up the limited foods available and was popular in working class areas. My favourite salad cream dish was mashed hard boiled eggs, salad cream and chopped chives in a wholemeal bread sandwich.

Salad cream sales declined in the 1970s, when American mayonnaise arrived in our shops as it seemed a more sophisticated product. In the 1990s, I wrote a cookery leaflet with 21 Heinz salad cream recipes. My family despaired at having to eat salad cream with nearly everything but the recipes worked well and it is a versatile ingredient.

The chef Marco Pierre White is supposed to have said 'Salad cream is one of the greatest culinary inventions.'

These are the food labels for salad cream and mayonnaise. The ingredients are the same, only in different proportions. Salad cream has half the calories of mayonnaise as mayonnaise has more oil. Both use pasteurised egg yolk for safety to avoid salmonella food poisoning.

Heinz salad cream 332 calories per 100g
Spirit Vinegar, Vegetable Oil (25%), Water, Sugar, Mustard, Salt, Egg Yolks (3%), Modified Cornflour, Stabilisers – Guar Gum and Xanthan Gum, Colour – Riboflavin.

Hellmann's mayonnaise 722 calories per 100g
Vegetable Oil (77%), Water, Pasteurised Egg & Egg Yolk (8%), Spirit Vinegar, Salt, Sugar, Lemon Juice, Mustard Flavouring, Antioxidant (Calcium Disodium EDTA), Paprika Extract.

The colour of egg shells

In the seventies, most of our eggs had white shells but gradually brown shelled eggs appeared in the shops and people thought they were healthier. In 2021, during the pandemic, white eggs were back in the supermarkets and sold for half the price of brown ones. The reason? Specific breeds of hen lay white eggs and these breeds can be kept in very large flocks as the hens are not as aggressive as brown egg laying hens. The white shelled eggs are therefore cheaper to produce and used by the food and catering industry. The pandemic closed many of these companies so there was a surplus supply of white eggs which supermarkets are selling at reduced prices. There is no nutritional difference between white and brown eggs.

The theory exam

In 1975, I joined the London Exam Board O level marking team and spoke out about inaccuracies and old fashioned questions. This was not well received. In 1979, I became Chief Examiner for the London Board cookery exams and set the questions and visited London schools to moderate their practical exams. Things changed fast. I included questions about new ingredients such as rice and pasta and cut down on the number of pastry and cake recipes they needed to practice. Questions like 'What do you serve with roast lamb?' were out. It was important to celebrate our diverse society through food.

The school flat

A gloomy print of The Chinese Girl by Vladimir Tretchikoff was hung in the school flat and we hated it. Her blue face seemed so miserable. Today a similar copy is for sale on eBay for £500. The original recently sold for £1 million. In the 1950s prints were bought from Boots for £1.

The picnic

Tupperware parties were a popular way to sell plastic storage pots in the UK from the 1960s. The Tupperware ladies who ran the parties had a strict dress code of skirts and stockings or tights to be worn at all times. The Tupperware host invites friends and neighbours to the party and gets free products like plastic bowls and storage containers in return. These parties stopped in the UK in 2003 – similar products could be bought from supermarkets.

Mark brought a bottle of Piat wine for us to sample at our picnic. French winemakers went on to create a brand called Le Piat D'Or from the original Piat as research showed this was a taste that people liked. This new wine had a consistent flavour that wine drinkers could rely on in the 1970s which was important as it could be a bit hit and miss when buying wine at that time. Le Piat D'Or had a great advertising campaign with the memorable line 'The French adore Le Piat D'Or' and it became a brand leader in the 1970s and 80s. So Mark was right – it did lead to big things.

Recipes from the 1970s

This is a sample of recipes that we cooked in school using inexpensive ingredients and margarine.

Prawn cocktail

To get the classic 1970's taste use readymade ingredients for the sauce – tomato ketchup and mayonnaise or salad cream. A squeeze of lemon – or, to be authentic, a squeeze of Jif Lemon – gives the sauce a lift. In the memory of H.E. Bates, an unpeeled prawn should be draped over the top of the serving glass.

Serves 4
Ingredients
200 g peeled prawns
3 tablespoons of mayonnaise or salad cream
1 tablespoon of tomato ketchup
Squeeze of lemon juice or Jif Lemon
Little Gem lettuce or floppy, tasteless 1970s lettuce
Paprika
Sprig of parsley
4 unpeeled prawns
Slice of brown bread and butter for each person, crusts removed and cut into quarters

Method

1. Mix the mayonnaise, ketchup and lemon juice and gently stir in the prawns.
2. Chop the lettuce into strips and put it in the bottom of 4 wine glasses.
3. Top each glass with the prawn mixture, sprinkle on a little paprika and put a sprig of parsley on top.
4. Drape an unpeeled prawn over the side of each glass.
5. Put the glass on a frilly d'oyley on a saucer and serve with quarters of buttered brown bread.

Soused herring

This recipe was part of the Fish lesson when students gutted and boned a herring which was not a job for the squeamish. Not a popular classroom dish.

Serves 4
Ingredients
4 herrings
1 small onion cut into rings
4 cloves
2 bay leaves
Vinegar and water in equal parts to cover the fish.

Method

1. Preheat the oven to 180°C/Gas 4.
2. Wash, trim and bone the fish.
3. Roll up the fish with some slices of onion and push the tail through the flesh like a fan.

4. Place in an ovenproof dish and add the cloves, bay leaves, vinegar and water, and cover with a lid or foil.
5. Bake in the oven for 30 minutes.
6. Serve warm or chilled.

Chicken liver patė

This recipe is made from chicken livers which are cheap and delicious and part of my Awful Offal lesson, trying to encourage students to like liver.

Serves 8

Ingredients

1 small onion, very finely chopped

60 g margarine or butter

2 crushed cloves garlic

250 g chicken livers – cut off the tubes

100 g bacon pieces, chopped

Salt and black pepper

1 tablespoons brandy – not allowed in the classroom.

Method

1. Fry the onion in 30 g of margarine or butter until soft but not coloured.
2. Add the garlic, chicken livers and bacon pieces and fry until cooked through, stirring all the time.
3. Season with salt and pepper then whizz in the food processor until smooth. Stir in the brandy if used. If you have no food processor, mash all the ingredients together with a fork to make a chunky patė.
4. Spoon the patė into a dish and pour over the remaining melted margarine or butter.
5. Leave to cool then chill in the fridge.
6. Serve with hot toast or crisp biscuits.

Spaghetti bolognese from the 70s

OK, I know this sounds horrid but this is my school recipe – if you want the real one, find a modern cookbook. In school minced beef was called mince but one student took home his recipe and wrote mice instead of mince. His mother wrote me a letter to check if he really needed to bring in some dead mice.

Serves 4
Ingredients
400 g minced beef
25 g lard
1 onion, finely chopped
3 tablespoons tomato ketchup
Pinch mixed herbs
100 g dried spaghetti
salt
50 g grated Cheddar cheese

Method

1. Fry the minced beef with the lard and chopped onion until the meat turns brown.
2. Stir in the tomato ketchup, mixed herbs and a little water to make a smooth sauce.
3. Cover the pan with a lid and cook gently for 10 minutes. Taste and season when cooked.
4. Half fill a large saucepan with boiling water.
5. Dip one end of the spaghetti in the water, wait until it softens, then wind the spaghetti around until it is completely covered by the water. Boil quickly for 10 minutes with the lid off, until the spaghetti is tender.
6. Throw it at the wall if you like. If it sticks it is done.
7. Drain off the water by pouring the contents through a colander which is held over a sink.

8. Place the spaghetti on a warm serving dish, pour the meat sauce over it and sprinkle grated cheese on top.

Baked stuffed lamb's hearts

Lamb's hearts are inexpensive and may be found in the freezer department of a supermarket. In 2021, two hearts cost £2 so that's £1 each. My students said that hearts were used as dog food and this seems to be true. The problem with this dish is that the hearts are still heart shaped when they come out of the oven. But some people love them. Lard was used for frying in the 1970s, but you can use vegetable oil.

Serves 4
Ingredients
1 onion, peeled and cut into slices
Knob of lard 25 g
4 lamb's hearts
Packet of sage and onion stuffing mix
20 g plain flour
500 ml boiling water
2 beef Oxo cubes

Method

1. Preheat the oven to 180°C/Gas 4.
2. Fry the onion in the lard in a frying pan until brown.
3. Prepare the hearts – remove the fatty bits and tubes that form the two pouches.
4. Make up the packet of stuffing mix according to instructions and press firmly into the hearts.
5. Fry the hearts with the onion slices and turn them until brown.
6. Remove the hearts and place in an ovenproof dish.

7. Stir the flour into the onions, slowly add the water and crumble in the Oxo cubes. Stir and cook until it thickens.
8. Pour the sauce over the hearts, cover with a lid or foil and bake in the oven for 1½ hours. Test to see if tender and if not cook for longer.
9. To serve, leave to stand for 10 minutes, then slice the hearts and cover with the gravy. Serve with creamy mashed potatoes.

Macaroni cheese

To increase the nutritional value and improve the colour I've added frozen peas to the basic recipe.

Serves 4

Ingredients

300 g dried macaroni

100 g frozen peas

30 g plain flour

30 g margarine or butter

300 ml milk – we used whole milk in the 1970s

150 g grated cheese – we used cheapest Cheddar, but strong matured Cheddar is good

½ teaspoon Colman's English Mustard Powder

White pepper

1 sliced tomato

Method

1. Preheat the oven to 190°C/Gas 5.
2. Cook the macaroni in boiling water until soft – see packet for instructions, but usually about 8 minutes. Add the frozen peas about 2 minutes before the end.

3. Make the white sauce by the all-in-one method – put the flour, margarine or butter and milk in a pan and whisk over the heat until the sauce thickens.
4. Stir in 100 g of the cheese and season with mustard and white pepper.
5. Drain the macaroni and peas and stir into the sauce.
6. Pile the mixture into an ovenproof dish and sprinkle the remaining cheese on top.
7. Decorate with a line of sliced tomato and bake in the oven for 20 minutes until the top is golden brown.

Angel Delight tart

This is a real packet mix dessert and to taste like the 1970s use Butterscotch or Strawberry flavour.

You can make your own pastry tart but the point of my lesson was to show how quick it was to cook using convenience food.

Serves 4

Ingredients

1 packet Angel Delight – Butterscotch or Strawberry flavour

Milk to mix

1 readymade pastry tart

Hundreds and thousands coloured sprinkles

Method

1. Prepare the Angel Delight according to packet instructions by mixing with milk.
2. Spoon the mixture into the ready made pastry tart case which is on a frilly d'oyley on a plate.
3. Leave to set in the fridge then scatter over the sprinkles and eat immediately. The colour runs out of the sprinkles if you

wait too long leaving streaks of rainbow colours across the dessert.

Brandy snaps

These golden, crispy rolls were sold at Wicksteed Park both in the tea room and wrapped in cellophane to take away. Work really quickly when the brandy snaps come out of the oven to roll them up when they are still warm.

Makes about 16

Ingredients

50 g margarine or butter

50 g granulated sugar

50 g plain flour

2 level tablespoons golden syrup

½ level teaspoon powdered ginger

Whipped cream

Glacé cherries

Method

1. Preheat the oven to 160°C/Gas 3.
2. Put the margarine or butter, sugar and syrup in a saucepan and heat slowly.
3. Beat in the flour and powdered ginger until smooth.
4. Line 2-3 baking trays with greased greaseproof paper or baking parchment.
5. Put teaspoons of the mixture on the tray, leaving 5 cm between each spoonful as the mixture spreads.
6. Bake for 8-12 minutes until the snaps are golden brown and bubbly.
7. Take out of the oven and leave for 2 minutes to cool, then remove one with a palette knife. Now work quickly. Wrap the snap around

the handle of a wooden spoon and hold it in place as it hardens. If the snaps get cold on the tray, warm them up in the oven.

8. Store the empty brandy snaps in an airtight tin away from other cakes as they absorb water.
9. When ready to serve fill one end with whipped cream and pop half a glacé cherry on top.
10. You can scatter the broken bits into plain Greek yogurt with chopped fruit to eat as a dessert.

Fairy cakes

This recipe only makes 6 cakes. In the classroom we made small quantities to keep down costs.

Makes 6

Ingredients

70 g soft margarine or butter
70 g caster sugar
1 large egg, beaten
70 g self raising flour
Vanilla essence
Icing sugar to make into glacé icing, or butter icing
Glacé cherry

Method

1. Preheat the oven to 190°C/Gas 5.
2. Beat the margarine or butter and sugar together with a wooden spoon until the mixture is pale and creamy and the sugar no longer feels gritty.
3. Beat the egg and add to the mixture adding some flour if the mixture shows signs of curdling.
4. Add the vanilla essence and then gently stir in the flour using a figure of eight if you wish.

5. Pile into six cake cases and bake for 15-20 minutes until the cakes are well risen and golden.
6. Cool and decorate with glacé icing and a glacé cherry.

Pineapple upside down cake

This is the prize dish that we progressed to when we learnt the creaming method.

Serves 6

Ingredients

125 g soft margarine or butter

125 g caster sugar

2 medium eggs, beaten

125 g self raising flour

Vanilla essence

25 g light brown sugar

Small can of pineapple rings, drained of juice

4 glacé cherries

Leaves of angelica

Method

1. Preheat the oven to 190°C/Gas 5.
2. Line a 20 cm cake tin with greased greaseproof paper to stop the mixture from sticking.
3. Sprinkle the light brown sugar in the base of the tin and arrange the pineapple rings to fit with a glacé cherry in the middle of each ring. Arrange some angelica leaves as decoration.
4. Beat the margarine or butter and sugar together with a wooden spoon until the mixture is pale and creamy and the sugar no longer feels gritty.
5. Beat the eggs and add to the mixture, adding some flour if the mixture shows signs of curdling.

6. Add the vanilla essence and then gently stir in the flour.
7. Spoon the sponge mixture on top of the pineapple rings and smooth down.
8. Bake for 20-30 minutes until the cake is golden and cooked. Insert a skewer to test if the mixture comes out clean when the sponge is cooked.
9. Turn out onto a large dish and serve as a pudding with custard, or as a cake. Heat the syrup from the juice from the can to make a sauce.

Cream horns

In the 1970s, we made rough puff pastry but it is easier to buy it ready rolled in a packet. Find cream horn tins on ebay, in antique shops or from catering suppliers.

Makes 10
Ingredients
320 g pack ready rolled puff pastry
Jam
Whipped cream
Sugar to sprinkle on pastry
Oil to grease cream horn tins

Method

1. Preheat the oven to 200°C/Gas 7.
2. Roll out the pastry from the packet and cut into thin strips 2x20cm long.
3. Dampen the pastry with water and wind round the tins starting at the pointed end and overlapping the strips.
4. Place on a non stick baking sheet with the joins of pastry tucked underneath.
5. Brush with sugar and water for the glaze.

6. Bake for 10 minutes, glaze again then bake a further 7-10 minutes until crispy and golden brown.
7. Leave to cool and carefully remove the pastry from the tins.
8. Spoon some jam into the pastry horn and fill with a little jam and whipped cream.

Acknowledgements

This memoir of teaching in the 1970s has taken fifteen years to write but COVID lockdown has given me time to complete. I'd like to thank Eleanor Fox, Sue Goodchild, Janet and Bryan Stuart who have patiently read the sections as they emerge from my dusty computer, and offered encouragement and advice. Many have shared memories of London fashions, restaurants, how we ate then and the challenges of teaching during that time. Thanks to Christine Thompson, Lesley Garner, Susan Johne, Linda Taylor, Jenny Cobley and Isobel Wilkinson.

Thankyou to Rebecca Perl of Messagelab Communications Ltd for editing and advice and Chloe King for designing the new website which clears the memories and clutter from my old site. And the Guild of Food Writers for answering so many questions.

Many people supported me along the way and I'd like to thank family and friends, and especially my grandmother who spent so much time with me sharing the joy of preparing fruits and vegetables from her garden.

Google has provided many insights and research for fact checking at a time when travel has been so limited, so thankyou to all the companies and people that post their memories and information. Marguerite Patten's book, *Cookery in Colour* was my bible when I was learning to cook and I visited her at home for tea and to check on my cooking facts. Why did we use fluted and plain flan rings, which d'oyley was correct, why the figure of eight to fold in flour? Seems like daft questions when there was so much to ask her.

I'd like to thank the students, whose names have all been changed for this memoir. One of them met me in the maternity ward of Whipps Cross Hospital when we were both giving birth and said 'Hello Miss.' I corrected her – there were nurses listening. 'It's Mrs, now.' In the 1970s it seemed important to be married when I had children. How times have changed.

And to all the food teachers who are working so hard at teaching the next generation of students how to cook. Well done – it's a very important subject and there's plenty of work for students.

Thanks to Simon Ridgwell for cover design, techie stuff and advice with promotion. His most important tip was to get on and write it to the best of my ability. Simon designed my Nutrition Program used by hundreds of schools and thousands of students learning about food and nutrition.

And finally to Mark. We went through a blip in 1972 which was the year of this memoir. He never knew about the other men in this story and he never will because he died in 2018. To quote Charlotte Bronte's famous line from Jane Eyre – 'Reader I married him' so it worked out in the end. He supported me for over fifty years when I was teaching in London schools, writing my textbooks, starting a business training food teachers around the country and producing resources for food education. One of his favourite dishes was stuffed lamb's hearts from my Awful Offal lesson which he really enjoyed when I tested the recipe for this book some years ago.

Jenny Ridgwell 2021

Summary

In 1970, I started teaching cooking in a north London comprehensive school, determined to share my passion for learning about food but I was faced with two mighty challenges. Firstly, keeping classroom discipline and secondly, the frustration of teaching out of date cooking skills with a large and diverse group of students. Exams tested traditional British baking skills and used textbooks written to train girls to become housewives.

After two years I became head of department in an east London comprehensive school and at twenty three I wanted to run things my way. It was the first time boys were allowed to choose cookery in my school and as the new teacher my register included students that no-one else wanted to teach.

Exams were the driving force and we worked through the seasons and preserved apples and onions in the autumn, made Christmas cakes, Seville orange marmalade in January, and prepared the first pink rhubarb in early spring. Shrove Tuesday was pancake day and the boys guffawed at learning the skill of tossing. They would josh and tease at the many rude words we had to learn about cooking.

The summer term brought the dreaded practical exam which tested us more than *The Great British Bake Off*. For two and a half hours they cooked a two course meal with all the trimmings, did some baking and for CSE exams carried out outdated tasks like starching and ironing a tray cloth. Their tables were laid with their cooking and an array of crockery, cruets sets, sauce boats and a flower arrangement. And they followed the d'oyley rule – plain d'oyleys for savoury and frilly for sweet.

Behind the scenes my private life was crumbling. Newly single, I moved into a dismal Hampstead bedsit and friends set about getting me off the shelf. At twenty three I was considered old to be looking for a partner. London was a playground for young people and there were plenty of food markets, wine bars, inexpensive restaurants and newly opened fashion shops to feast on.

This is a story of a memorable year starting in September 1972 and it's also a piece of social history. Life in Britain and especially London was changing fast. The seventies was a time of unrest and financial challenge for many and our food choices were changing with so many new ingredients like avocados and Angel Delight. It was the last year that students could leave at Easter when they reached sixteen so some left school with no qualifications and I wonder how they managed with nothing to prove what they could achieve – this made them challenging to teach.

Many people supported me along the way and I'd like to thank family and friends, and especially my grandmother who spent so much time with me sharing the joy of preparing fruits and vegetables from her garden.

The cookery exams at the time drove me mad as the questions were written for girls and housewives and I railed against the exam boards to change. Eventually I became a chief examiner and was able to set my own questions and curriculum.

The textbooks we used had astonishing facts that no-one seems to have checked – vegetarian food was described as difficult to prepare and missing the flavours of meat and fish. They had to learn stuff like which sauce to serve with lamb or beef which in multicultural London made no sense. Most of the lessons that I taught became part of a new textbook commissioned by Oxford University Press, called *Finding Out About Food*. My editor wanted to include some daft things I'd taught like rolling an egg on the floor to see how it came back and we had recipes like spaghetti bolognese made with tomato ketchup. *Food Around the World* was my next school textbook so I was able to research many recipes and stories from the mixed communities where I'd taught.

My passion for food continues and I set up my own company training food teachers in the ever-changing challenges of education. Since 1980 I've written over seventy textbooks and set up The Nutrition Program which students use to analyse recipes, diets and meals.

Jenny Ridgwell 2021

A review from Christine Thompson

I have known Jenny since the 1990s through my work as a Food Adviser/Inspector for a large County and worked closely with Jenny on her many successful courses. On my visits to schools at this time her textbooks and courses were the main source that teachers grew on for inspiration in their teaching. I regularly met secondary heads of food departments after school to discuss updates and many travelled miles to come to share experiences and ideas. If they knew Jenny would be there, whole departments would voluntarily attend. When Jenny was writing new material she was keen to capture the teachers' opinion before publication and many trialled her work giving her detailed evaluation of their findings which she listened to and took on board.

One of her many successes has been the development of the Nutrition Program for schools. It's ease of use on schools IT networks was at the forefront of technology. Jenny is held in high regard by teachers and students not only in this country but around the world. Her books are still being printed and used and she continues to work on new material and updated earlier editions.

The experience Jenny gained teaching Food subjects in the 1970s led her to challenge the thinking of the establishment at that time by writing modern textbooks and involving herself with the Examination Boards. Within a short period of time she became a chief examiner. She went on to inspire and influence change when food education was not given the respect it deserved. It was based on outdated ideas of a past age.

Since then she has continued to publish many textbooks and successfully run courses for teachers round the country based on meticulous research ensuring that every detail was based on evidence.

Teachers and students have a lot to thank Jenny for her lifelong dedication to Education.

Christine Thompson Hampshire Inspector for Design and Technology from 1992 – 1998 Ofsted Inspector for Design and Technology 1995 – 2007

Christine Thompson is a great supporter of food education, and inspired and helped me run many training courses for food education around the country.

Printed in Great Britain
by Amazon

71475846R00119